How to modify
BMW E30
3 SERIES
for high-performance & competition

This book is dedicated to Diana and Peter, and all the adventures yet to come.

T0386281

www.veloce.co.uk

First published in September 2013, reprinted November 2021 by Veloce Publishing Limited, Veloce House, Parkway Farm Business Park, Middle Farm Way, Poundbury, Dorchester, Dorset, DT1 3AR, England. Tel 01305 260068/Fax 01305 250479/e-mail info@veloce.co.uk or www.veloce.co.uk/web www.velocebooks.com.
ISBN: 978-1-845844-38-7 UPC: 6-36847-04438-1

Readers with ideas for automotive books, or books on other transport or related hobby subjects, are invited to write to the editorial director of Veloce Publishing at the above address.
British Library Cataloguing in Publication Data – A catalogue record for this book is available from the British Library.
Typesetting, design and page make-up all by Veloce Publishing Ltd on Apple Mac. Printed and bound by CPI Group (UK) Ltd, Croydon, CR0 4YY.

How to modify

BMW E30

3 SERIES

for high-performance & competition

Ralph Hosier

VELOCE PUBLISHING
THE PUBLISHER OF FINE AUTOMOTIVE BOOKS

Contents

CONTENTS

Introduction & about this book

INTRODUCTION

The word 'icon' is used far too much these days. In the world of cars, there are in reality only a few true icons, such as the E-Type and the original Mini, and surely the BMW E30 3 Series ranks among them. Its classic quad-light, kidney-shaped grille front end is instantly recognisable as pure BMW, an image featured in many stylised art shots, on magazine covers, posters, and even T-shirts.

But it's not just an image – it's a package that really delivers, too.

The splendid thing about the E30 is how easy it is to turn into a fairly swift racer. The shell is a good compromise between strength and lightness, the engine is robust and tunable, and of course, the suspension is legendary. As I write this book prices are still quite low, making it possible to build a good budget racer with performance and handling to beat some very expensive competition. A fabulous example of budget racing and utter giant killing is the story of Bill Caswell's E30: a $500 wreck of a car built economically, which went on to successfully compete in a round of the World Rally Championship. If you don't know the story, I strongly suggest you search for 'Bill Caswell's E30' on the web; chances are he will have done something else amazing with it!

But times are changing. Older cars are either being scrapped or restored, in some cases at great expense, so the pool of affordable solid cars is slowly drying up, and prices are inevitably going to rise. So, my friends, now is the time!

ABOUT THIS BOOK

In this book I explore popular tuning methods and techniques, from a light tune-up to a full-blown racing car spec, and most things in between. Chapter one gives a short history lesson, just to provide a flavour of the development this iconic car has received over the years. At the end of the book I cover a few case studies – it's always interesting to see which modifications work in real life, and maybe get a little inspiration.

I give an overview of the options available for tuning and modifying these great cars, detailing the relative merits of each method, and the difficulties most commonly encountered. This is not a workshop manual – there are already many excellent ones around – but the book provides you with enough detail to make informed decisions and inspire your imagination.

Special thanks to:

Peter Lightfoot for use of his E30 in many of the pictures. He runs Petrol Threads, and makes superb car-related T-shirts – his E30 shirt is a firm favourite of ours. Please look at: http://petrolthreads.co.uk

Major James Cameron who supplied many of the pictures here, and created the amazing M30-powered racer in chapter five. He also runs a fantastic charity that helps disabled service personnel recover by using motorsport to develop skills and confidence. Please take a moment to look at www.missionmotorsport.org

Lee Marshall provided some fantastic pictures of our E30s on track. If you do a trackday at an MSV circuit, you will find his pictures of your car at www.clubmsvphotography.com

A very special thanks to BMW UK, which very kindly gave permission for me to use its pictures. Look at its new car specs and play with its configurator at www.bmw.co.uk

WARNING
Modifying cars is dangerous!

In fact, cars are dangerous in the first place, and modifying critical parts can turn them into death traps if done badly. Before undertaking any work on your car make sure you have the right skills and qualifications. There is absolutely no excuse for ignorance these days, as there are so many excellent and affordable courses at colleges, so even those without technical backgrounds can get properly trained.

In this book I cover a huge range of modifications, but just because someone else has successfully performed a modification does not mean that it will automatically work on your car – check that what you plan to do is a good idea before changing anything on your car.

Also, in any book there is always the possibility that something has been misprinted or is plain wrong; don't take everything as certain fact. Obviously I work hard to ensure everything I write is correct, and many of the modifications here I have tried myself, but there is always the potential for errors.

If you have any doubts about a modification or of your own ability to do it, DON'T DO IT!

The E30 doing what it does best: entertaining the driver (in this case, the author). (Courtesy Lee Marshall)

Chapter 1
History

The E30 followed on from the E21 3 Series, which had largely introduced the world to the distinctive BMW 'shark nose' styling. The E30 carried over many of the E21 fundamentals, but with detail changes that transformed the handling, performance, and quality. Very few parts were carried over without revision – even the engine block was recast to be lighter. The wheelbase was 7mm longer, the track was just over a centimetre wider, and it was slightly roomier inside, but the weight remained roughly the same. It was evolution rather than revolution, building on the strengths of the E21 and learning the lessons. This made a better engineered solution, but the downside was that when the E30 was launched it already looked dated compared to the 'jelly mould' Ford Sierra or low drag Audi 100.

From a performance tuning point of view, some of the detail changes made the E30 a significantly better car, such as using the 'boomerang' lower wishbone at the front, rather than the combination of anti-roll bar and track control arm on the E21 that

formed a lower wishbone. The use of combined roll bar and track arm was very common at the time, but although it worked well enough for most road car applications, it did introduce a touch too much compliance, which allowed the wheel to change position inadvertently when driven very hard. BMW was not forced to improve this system, but did anyway, setting the company on a different path to the more cost-focussed competitors. The result is very accurate wheel control, which is one of the many reasons the car became so popular and successful at racing, winning many championships and even doing fairly well at rallying. Although the camber change from the rear suspension made it more suitable to flatter tracks such as gravel or tarmac rallies, it still makes a very usable forest rally car when fitted with the right LSD.

It was also one of the first cars of that era to take build quality seriously. While other manufacturers had been concentrating on reducing costs, sometimes to the detriment of longevity and functionality, BMW went the other

Simple and utilitarian, the E30 was designed as a family car for the mass market. This 316i is typical.

way. The doors fitted the holes properly – which at the time was not always the case with other manufacturers – so wind noise was reduced, and the well-designed door seals contributed to a positive sound when closing the door, making the car feel solid. All cars corrode, and at that time some cars would need substantial welding after just five years, but although the E30 was not immune to corrosion, the combination of thicker paint and good body design made it last a lot longer

The light weight and fine handling inevitably resulted in high-performance models, like this M3.

Large, powerful engines in modestly-priced cars, such as this 325i, inspired generations to convert E30s into track and race cars.

The mechanical parts and basic chassis also spawned many spin-off models, such as this Z1.

than its competitors, helping create the reputation of BMW quality.

The E30 was launched first as a 323i, and the first customers received cars in December 1981. From the very first test drive it was clear something special had arrived, though it was by no means perfect. One criticism was the lack of leg and head room in the rear, so in 1983 the rear foot-wells were lowered and the seatback sculpted deeply. Curiously, the steering rack was designed with a huge number of turns lock to lock: 3.9 for the power steering variants and 4.8 for the unassisted models. Compare this to the Morris Minor, which needed less than three, yet had a near identical turning circle.

Initially, engine performance was also a bit disappointing for the price, the 323 having 139bhp yet costing a lot more than a Ford Capri 2.8i with 160bhp. These issues were soon addressed, and the E30 became recognised as a real driver's car. It was one of the few cars available at the time with a 6-cylinder engine in a lightweight shell. Whilst other companies such as Triumph had tried this, none had a big engine coupled with accurate suspension and a stiff shell. It is also worth mentioning that BMW South Africa locally produced a 333i with the 3.3-litre big six engine, as seen in the 633 of the time. Interestingly, it later replaced this with the small six, using the 2.7 Eta block, but with 325 '888'

heads and its own cams. The '325is' eventually produced more power than the original 333i, which goes some way to demonstrating the potential of the small six engine.

However, many cars used the 4-cylinder engines, which were still quite powerful for that era. To begin with, the M10 engine was used. First introduced in the 2002 back in the late '60s, this fine small engine has had an amazing career in motorsport. Making about 300bhp in full race trim and winning many races at the time, including Touring Car, it also formed the basis for the turbocharged F1 engine that gave over 1200bhp in qualifying trim, and the block was later used in the M3's S14 engine. In the E30, the M10 was initially introduced as a carburettor engine, but later had the fuel-injection system fitted, similar to the 6-cylinder engines. The M10 was replaced later by the M40 engine with a belt-driven cam, which was a bit more powerful and had better emissions and economy, although lacked some of the low-speed torque. This was superseded by the M42 chain-driven cam engine in the last 318is, an engine that carried on into the E36.

The racing version of the M42 engine, the S42, was used in BMW's 320 four-door entry in the German STW (Super TourenWagen) race series. Featuring individual throttle bodies with eight fuel injectors, a carbon fibre valve cover and airbox, dry sump lubrication

system, higher compression ratio, and a capacity of 1999cc, it produced up to 315bhp.

When the M division took on the task of producing a homologation special, it chose to tune the M10 4-cylinder engine. The lower weight would allow the car to handle corners far more easily than the iron blocked six, resulting in faster lap times on race circuits. Initially it was taken to 2.3 litres, but the Sport Evolution took it to 2.5 and 238bhp. It had unique 16-valve heads similar in design to the M88 6-cylinder engine, and used four individual throttle bodies. A short-stroke version of this engine was made for the 320is specifically for the Portuguese and Italian markets, where its 2.0-litre capacity gave it a much lower tax value than the 325. These can make excellent race engines, if you can find them.

It is very interesting to look at the differences between the standard E30 and the M3. The usual racing formula was followed by widening the track and using bigger brakes and wheels, plus the bodywork was modified with wide arches and aerodynamic tweaks to improve high-speed stability and traction. Although the M3 used a standard two-door E30 bodyshell, the only external panels that remained standard were the roof and bonnet. The standard shell is a very good basis for tuning.

A lot of the lessons learnt from the M3 were implemented for the E30's replacement, the E36, including the 5-bolt hubs and the E28-derived 5 Series struts and brakes. The E36 was an evolution, and so provides a wealth of engine and suspension upgrade opportunities for the E30.

The E30 also donated some parts to the Z1 sports car, launched in 1987. It used the 325i E30 engine and gearbox, canted over slightly for the low bonnet line, and widened suspension similar to the M3 at the front, but a Z link rear similar to the forthcoming E36.

The E30 rear axle still lived on, though. It was used in the short E36 Compact due to its small size, and also on the Z3 and M Coupé.

The final years of E30 production overlapped its successor, the E36. The Cabriolet and Touring models continued until suitable replacements based on the E36 were developed.

TIMELINE

1982 (1981 – 323i)
The E30 3 Series launched in Germany as 316 (carburetted 1.8-litre M10), 318i (injected 1.8-litre M10), 320i (M20), and 323i (M20). Improved handling over the E21 prompts good reviews. The Baur Cabriolet offered by dealers.

1983
UK launch with right-hand drive. Revisions to rear seat and footwell improve rear space.

North America receives the 325e with a 2.7-litre M20 engine tuned for low-speed torque and fuel efficiency, capable of 40mpg. Sold in Europe from '85, but not officially in the UK.

1984
South Africa receives the 333i with the larger 3.3-litre M30 engine.

1985
The 323i is replaced by the range-topping 325i. The four-wheel drive 325ix aimed mainly at the Scandinavian and other snowy territories, brought the BMW brand to a new audience. The first BMW diesel, the 324d with the M21 based on an M20 block, introduced with a pedestrian 86bhp.

1986
M3 performance derivative launched with 2.3-litre version of the S14 4-cylinder engine, wider track, bigger brakes, improved handling, and extensive body modifications for styling and improved aerodynamics.

BMW in-house convertible offered alongside the cheaper Baur Cabriolet. The rear wheelarches were redesigned to accommodate the hood, making them lower than other models. This was later applied to the whole range.

1987
The E30 range had a face lift, new integrated plastic bumpers made the cars look a little more modern and the lower rear wheelarch design, first seen on the factory convertibles, was carried over to the whole range.

The old M10 engine is finally replaced by the M40 4-cylinder engine with belt-driven cam in the 318i

The 324d is joined by a turbo-diesel version; 324td with 113bhp.

1988
The 316i receives a 1.6-litre version of the M40 engine.

M3 Cabriolet and 3 Series Touring estate car launched.

New 'smiley' headlamps with a curved cutout and ellipsoid lamps introduced.

1989
The 318is is launched with a 16-valve M42 4-cylinder engine generating 136bhp.

South Africa receives the 325is, which, unlike the 2.5-litre 325is in other markets, has the 2.7-litre M20 tuned to 197bhp, later upped to 210bhp in 1991.

1990
M3 Evo III now has a 2.5-litre version of the S14 engine.

1991
Although the E36 is launched and E30 Saloon production stops, the Touring (now also available as the 316i) and convertible E30 variants continue.

1993
Production of the convertible ends.

1994
The final E30 Touring is produced, marking the end of E30 production. However, E30 parts continue in production for use in the E36 Compact and Z3 until 2002.

BMW MODEL NUMBERS
BMW uses a three digit number for the E30 cars. The first digit is the model range, and the last two usually give an indication of engine size, but not always. BMW took the view that most people think of the engine size being proportional to performance, so it used the last two digits as a relative indication of the car's performance compared to other models in the range. So, whilst the 325i was indeed a 2.5-litre engine, the 325e was in fact a 2.7-litre tuned for high economy and low end torque, and so had comparable performance to the 325i. Similarly, the original 316 was in fact a 1.8-litre M10 engine, but in a lower state of tune to the same engine in the 318. Confusingly, later 316 cars actually did have a 1.6-litre M40 engine.

Chapter 2

Buying a project car

Undoubtedly the most crucial aspect in any project is the starting point. Pick a good car, and it's all smiles; pick a bad one, and you will spend more time fixing other people's mistakes than you will doing the jobs you had planned.

The ideal base car depends on what you are aiming to achieve. Some race formulas require a specific model to be eligible, and even if you are building a road car, some models offer more potential than others. Ultimately, budget is a major consideration, and for a given price it can be better to get a less-than-ideal model in a good condition, rather than buying a more desirable model in a rotten state.

Many people also buy a second rotten car just to harvest spare parts. Indeed, I have done exactly that in the past myself, when I bought a sound 316i two-door and a rotten 325i for the engine and gearbox, but there are a few traps with this approach. There was a face-lift in about 1987 that involved a number of detail changes to the shell, making some swaps a little more tricky. For instance, I found the radiator

Well-proportioned and logically laid out, the interior is easy to use and accommodates a wide range of drivers.

Slim by modern standards, the E30 should fit most garages, and won't embarrass the driver in the car park.

mounts and the mounting points for the prop centre bearing were completely different, necessitating fabricating adaptors and new brackets. So, if you are going to buy a scrapper for parts, just make sure it's compatible with your project car.

If you are buying a car for trackday

Unfinished projects can be a bargain buy, but more often they are unfinished for a very good reason! If buying a non-runner, make sure you can transport it home.

The E30 is easy to live with and fun to use, bringing a smile to the face of any car lover.

It won't be long before new friends come over to share the fun.

The next issue is mechanical failure of over-stressed standard parts, and electrical gremlins as connectors and wires are tested by vibrations and G-forces. So, some of the key items to consider are ease of servicing and availability of spare parts, and this is where the high-performance versions of many cars can prove unwise buys.

Let me explain using the ever-popular M3 as an example. If you are going to prepare a car for regular track use, you might strip out the interior to save weight, fit lowered and stiffened suspension, a race seat, maybe a spoiler and splitter etc. But the M3 differed from the standard 325 in precisely these ways – it had slightly lower and stiffer suspension, subtle but important modifications to the aerodynamics, sports seats, and 5 Series-derived wheels and brakes. Most of these exclusive and expensive M parts are to some extent superfluous if the car is going to be converted anyway. It could work out a whole lot easier to start with a good quality standard 325i and fit the track/race parts to that instead. This is also important if you are on a tight budget – buying a top condition cheaper model will make a much more reliable car than buying a rot box example of a top spec car.

And of course if your car is a standard model parts will be cheaper and you will have a lot less investment tied up in it, so you will be a lot less worried about pushing it to the limits, which means more fun factor.

Success comes from simplicity.

THE 4- OR 6-CYLINDER ENGINE?

The higher power of the 6-cylinder engines is always going to be tempting, but the M division's view was that the 4-cylinder engine's lower weight made it the better choice for racetrack success and road driving pleasure. Another interesting example is the Performance BMW Championship race series which allows four and 6-cylinder engines. The 4-cylinder is slightly better in corners,

fun, you are best off getting something reliable – it's amazing how many cars don't make it past lunchtime on a full day event. Many people make the mistake of buying something quite complicated that is simply overwhelmed by the rigours of going flat-out for long stretches of time. It's usually heat that causes most problems, in the cooling systems, transmission and the brakes.

Its racing pedigree means the E30 shines on the track – a great place to experience its true potential. (Courtesy Lee Marshall)

All classics need repair at some point. Luckily, the E30 is easy to work on, and spare parts are readily available.

and the six is slightly better on the straights.

In many respects the best engine depends on what you intend to do with the car, and also on your budget. A cheap trackday car will work well with the standard 2.5-litre 6-cylinder engine, but a 4-cylinder may provoke you into spending time and money tuning it. It all depends on your preference.

If you have the money, then maybe a turbocharged 4-cylinder could be the ultimate E30. After all, the original 4-cylinder in the E30 was the M10 engine, which is related to the legendary F1 turbo engine of the '80s that managed 1200bhp (briefly) in qualifying trim! However, that was with colossal budgets.

LIST OF COMMON MODELS

The E30 Saloon started production in December 1981, arrived in the UK in March 1983, and was in production until 1991. The estate Touring arrived in 1988, and continued in production until 1994, some four years after the E36 Coupé had begun to replace the E30 Coupé.

Initially the E30 was offered with the old 4-cylinder M10 engine in 1.8-litre form with injection or carburettors. These are very tough old engines that have been used since 1961 and offer a lot of tuning potential. They were used in top level motorsport, including Touring Car, so a generous amount of tuning parts are available.

The M10 was superseded by the M40 engine with a belt driven cam, which strangely has less tuning

The early 4-cylinder cars can offer good value – they are engaging to drive and easy to maintain. Note the steel bumper with chrome trim used on pre-face-lift cars.

The smaller-engined 6-cylinder cars are often cheaper, but still offer great enjoyment.

The 325i is probably the most popular model now – excellent performance, even by modern standards.

The four-door models are sometimes cheaper than the rarer two-door models. Remember to check all locks and handles, as the rear doors are frequently neglected.

potential, partly due to some fragility in the head, but largely because it was not extensively used in motorsport, so there are fewer tuning parts available. This was partly due to the introduction of the final iteration of the 4-cylinder E30: the M42 engine with chain-driven cams. It first saw production in the 318is and continued into the E36, its twin-cam heads offer a fair amount of potential and there are many tuning parts available.

The 6-cylinder models had the 'small six,' available in 2.0, 2.3, and 2.5-litre forms, and was a carryover from the E21 in many respects, although many details were changed, and even the block castings were lighter and stronger. This is a good solid engine, and the 2.0-litre revs very well indeed,

making it suitable for many 2.0-litre classes in racing. The 2.3 was a bit of a halfway house, making it a less appealing to many, but usually this means they are cheaper to buy and so a good 323 could make a sound trackday project if budgets are tight. The most popular six is the 2.5-litre – it's relatively easy to get over 200bhp without too much expense. The popularity is reflected in prices, though, and some fairly poor examples are presented as being something special by over-optimistic sellers.

RARE MODELS

The most famous is the M3, which went through several changes starting with a 2.3-litre version of the M10 engine, known as the S14B23, and finishing with a 2.5-litre version known as the S14B25. They had extensive revisions to suspension, drivetrain, interior and bodywork. Of the outer panels, only the roof and bonnet are shared with the usual E30. Prices have been rising for many years, and they have become firm favourites of collectors and investors. Their value now makes their use as a

trackday car base questionable. Also, the rarity of the body panels means that any damage will become increasingly difficult to repair. They are, however, a very well sorted car as standard, and as they formed the basis of BMW's Touring Car program in the early '90s, there are a lot of tuning specialists available to squeeze even more performance out of the chassis and engine, for a price.

Another rare version is the Baur Cabriolet. Baur took standard E30 cars from BMW and rebuilt them with its own roof system and extensive body modifications. They were sold through the BMW dealer network, and are therefore considered equivalent to the BMW factory models. Other than the roof and body modifications, the car was a standard E30, so service parts are not a problem. However, roof parts are becoming harder to find, and any damaged parts may have to be repaired rather than replaced.

An interesting rarity is the four-wheel drive 325ix model. Made between 1988 and 1991, it had a transfer box fitted to a special gearbox casing, and the front differential mounted on

The 1987 face-lift brought plastic bumpers and improved front 'chin.' This example's headlights have the washer-wipers and the 'smiley' cutouts.

Later 4-cylinder models offer reasonable fuel economy and sprightly performance.

The convertible can be a joy to drive in the right conditions. These are not the right conditions, but they still offer huge fun.

BMW using an E30 for driver training. (Courtesy BMW)

The M3 had substantial differences from other models. Completely different wings with wider arches, special front and rear spoilers, and a lower rear window angle. Some still regard the original M3 as the best ever made.

The M3 became an icon of performance motoring. (Courtesy BMW)

a unique front crossmember, with the right-hand driveshaft passing through a tube in the special sump. Because of the extra machinery on the right, the car was only made in left-hand drive.

Suspension geometry was changed to suit the fact that the front wheels were now pulling the car along too. The unique front struts had shorter dampers because of the fork-shaped structure at the lower end needed to go around the driveshaft, and the track width was increased to accommodate the drive shafts. Even the wheels had greater offsets to compensate. The front wheels were set slightly more toe-out to make the car safer for novices on snowy roads, which does blunt the usual E30 steering sharpness, but is easily altered.

There are a myriad of other special variants, such as the BMW South Africa 333 and 327, the Alpina range,

Open top motoring with exhilarating performance. (Courtesy BMW)

Beware modified cars. Whilst there are many excellent examples, there are also a large number of amateur conversions with potential safety problems.

Check the lights work and that there is no residue inside the lens. Look through the grille to check the integrity of the radiator. Check the front bumper and trim is secure.

and also the 2.0-litre M3 sold in Italy and Portugal. Their rarity makes them unlikely choices for a modified car, although you never know what might turn up as a 'barn find' bargain.

INSPECTION CHECK LIST

First check the service history. The first thing to look for is that the timing belt on M20 and M40 engines has been changed at the recommended intervals. Ideally, the water pump should also have been changed, and for M20 engines the later type of idler fitted.

Exterior

Check the bumpers are fitted securely. Mountings corrode, and if a bumper has been removed previously the bolts may have broken. Also, the chrome trim is prone to corrosion. If there is any bubbling on top then it may well be worse underneath.

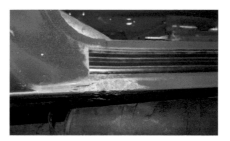

Sills and floor corners are the most likely rust spots. If possible, look behind/under carpets and trim.

Rust is always a problem, E30s suffer rot in all four corners of the floorpan, usually near the sill – it's definitely worth pulling the carpet back to have a quick look. Don't rely on looking at it from underneath, as many models have underseal that will mask even quite large patches of rust.

Look under the lower edge of the sills where they join the floor. Push the panels with the probing tool to check for rust behind the underseal. Look along

Cabrio tops can leak. Check there are no gaps when the roof is up.

the sills and push them with gloved hands. Check the jacking points for corrosion and see if they are misshapen. Push the front and rear parts of the rear wheelarches too. Both these areas are repairable, but involve a fair amount of cutting and welding, so if you are not planning on doing it yourself it could prove expensive.

Press the lower corners of the windscreen surround, which can rust from the inside. Look at the paint

White water vapour when starting a cold engine on a cold day is normal, but grey or blue smoke indicates possible engine wear. Whilst at the back of the car, check the lights, lock and boot for corrosion.

Check all the switches work, including those for windows. Ensure the dash warning lights work.

carefully – is it original? Look inside the engine bay for tell-tale signs of previous different paint colours. Use the magnet to check the wings are steel and not filler.

The door gaps (shut lines) should be uniform width, with no paint chips on the edge.

Headlights can suffer from a milky build-up inside, which is difficult to shift. Also the light mounting brackets suffer from rot and the adjustment screws corrode so that adjustment can become impossible.

The numberplate area on the boot suffers, particularly around the mounting holes. Whilst in the boot take off the rear light covers and check for rust at the mounting points.

Interior
The edge of the driver's seat suffers the most wear, and is an indication of the car's mileage.

Feel the carpet at the four corners – damp often means the floor has rusted out.

If the car is for concourse and show purposes, makes sure the interior is all original. Finding genuine trim parts to rectify any problems can be very difficult, as they are no longer made, and stocks of secondhand parts are limited.

Cloth and leather can be repaired to some extent, and cracks in plastic

parts can be welded in most cases, but to get good results you'll need to pay an expert.

Pull out the seat belts fully and check for damaged threads, which will weaken the belt severely. Also check the buckle mechanism works properly.

Check all the electric windows work. If the cutout has popped out, press it in and see if all the windows work without it popping again.

Recline the front seats – the gear drive and strut can wear, becoming loose.

Check all the door locks including the boot, using all the keys. Remote locking often means locks never get used, and seize up.

Run through all the switch functions including headlights, indicators, and horn. Also check the interior heater fan works.

Mechanicals
Under the bonnet the engine should be free of oil stains and aluminium corrosion, and the engine bay should be clean, but beware recently steam-cleaned spotless examples on all but concourse models – it may have just been done to conceal oil leaks.

The engine oil should be between min and max marks and be golden in colour; black oil is a bad sign. Look into the cam cover under the oil filler cap. The metal of the rocker shafts should be olive or golden in colour; black sludge

Assess the condition of the interior. The outer edge of the driver's seat usually gets the most wear, and often starts ripping at around 100,000 miles.

Check for damaged or cracked hoses in the engine bay, and listen for rattling or knocking from the engine. Check the fluids are clean and topped up.

indicates long-term neglect, white or yellow 'mayonnaise' indicates oil and water contamination.

When you first see the car, check the engine is cold. Feel the rocker cover for warmth; if the car has been warmed up before you get there, it could mean the vendor is trying to cover cold starting problems.

Rubber on cars generally starts cracking up within ten years, so look for hardening and tiny cracks on coolant, oil, and fuel hoses. The rubber intake ducts between the airbox and throttle

Check beneath the engine for leaks, if possible. This one shows a small leak from the front of the engine, which will compromise the cam belt.

Turning the steering to full lock allows a glimpse of the brakes and suspension. There should be no slack in the ball joints.

Looking through the wheel spokes, the brake disc should have little rust and should not have wear grooves.

Take a look underneath. Some oil staining is normal, but it should not be dripping.

age and crack, which results in stalling or poor idle. Check all round and give it a squeeze.

Whilst the bonnet is open, check the VIN plate and engine numbers match the log book, and check for paint over-spray on the VIN plate too, which indicates a hasty respray. The VIN plate should be secure with no gap underneath – if it has been removed or is off another vehicle, it may sit very slightly proud of the bodywork.

Also look under the battery tray. Acid may have been spilt, which removes the paint and lets rot start.

Look at the state of the brake disks through the wheel spokes. Tug at the track rods to check for looseness, and bounce the corners to see if the dampers are worn. Chances are you will replace these parts anyway, but spotting worn parts may help in negotiating a better price.

As ever, the suspension and hub bearings should be checked by giving the top of the wheel a very firm pull and push, although this will only show a problem if the wear is particularly severe.

With the key in position one, wiggle the steering wheel and listen for any loose joints clonking. There should be almost no free play.

On the test drive

One key thing is to check the speedo works, and crucially that the mileage (odometer) increases as you drive, otherwise the recorded mileage is meaningless.

Allow the engine to get to normal working temperature and then let it idle for a few minutes. Worn ignition parts or badly adjusted fuelling will result in a

Unladen, the rear is slightly higher than the front as standard.

Springs break. Stand back a fair way and look at how the car sits. If it's leaning to one side, expect trouble.

Corrosion lurks behind the rear lights, at the edge of the boot (trunk) lid and boot floor, and at the towing point. This example is beautifully sound.

misfire or unstable idle eventually. This also ensures the fan and thermostat are working properly. If the temperature keeps climbing, then obviously stop before it overheats!

The steering should be light once on the move, with no play. Vibration could mean unbalanced or buckled wheels. If very gentle braking causes steering vibration, it could mean the brake discs are warped. If the car pulls to one side there could be a number of causes, including tyre pressure, tyre type, bent chassis, or suspension.

At steady speed, back off the power and then immediately back on. This puts a jolt through the transmission and helps to reveal worn engine mounts, gearbox mounts, prop centre bearing, prop joints, and half-shaft wear. Also try to find a stretch of rough road and listen for suspension noises caused by worn bushes or ball joints.

Check the general condition of the engine bay. Arriving for a test drive and finding the engine already warm and steam-cleaned should raise questions.

The view many drivers wish for. A well laid-out and easy to use interior adds to the driving pleasure. (Courtesy BMW)

Seats are firm but supportive, if in good condition. Styling is very '80s. (Courtesy BMW)

The sort of road the E30 excels on. (Courtesy BMW)

Chapter 3

Common faults, servicing & recommissioning

COMMON FAULTS
Paint

Take a careful look along the panels, getting your eye close to the paint so you can see any irregularities more clearly. Look inside the engine bay for tell-tale signs of previous different paint colours.

BMW seemed to suffer from poor quality lacquer that blisters and allows paint to oxidise. A temporary remedy is to cut back the edges of the damaged area with rubbing compound and then spray spots of new lacquer on. This will stop the underlying paint getting further damage, but only looks good from a distance! This may be fine for a trackday hack, but if you care about appearance then the only proper solution is a full respray.

Panels

Use the magnet to check the wings are steel, not filler.

Rust is a common problem at the four corners of the floorpan. If possible, lift the corners of the carpet to check for dampness, and look at the floor

Try to look across panels so that objects with straight lines, such as fences, reflect in the paint. This highlights any irregularities.

Check wings for filler and rot. This car has been lowered and the tyre has caught the edge of the arch, pulling it out.

The 'A' pillars and windscreen surround are prone to rust. Look carefully around the seal edge for bubbling or lifting caused by underlying rot.

Floor corners are another rot-spot. Look under carpets if possible. If the accelerator pedal is loose at the lower end, it may be due to rust under the hinge.

Sill edges and joins to the floor have a hard life. Use a gloved hand or a probe to check for rust behind underseal.

The rear valance near the towing eye and above the exhaust can corrode. Check the bumper and exhaust are secure.

The convertible hood is a complex system, and linkages can become twisted or loose. Check it opens and closes correctly.

The battery may be located in the boot or engine bay. Check underneath it for rust. Also make sure the earth strap connections are in good condition. The spare wheel well can rot where moisture collects.

underneath. A small amount of surface rust can be simply treated, but flakes of deep-seated rust may need sections of floor to be cut out and new sections welded in.

As with most cars, the sills on an E30 take a battering from debris thrown up by the wheels, which chips away at the paint and underseal. Moisture gets trapped in the lower seam joint. Later

models had a galvanised front valance panel, but stone chips and road salt will still corrode this item. Replacement is

The shut lines should be of even width all the way down. Check doors, bonnet, and boot lid, plus the sunroof if fitted.

If you want original looks, check all the trim parts are present and secure. This car has missing rubbing strips, which are getting harder to find in good condition.

BMW roundels are prime targets for thieves. If the plastic begins separating from the back it will become opaque and the logo may deteriorate.

reasonably straightforward, and panels are still available.

The rear valance on the right-hand side near the towing eye traps water and corrodes.

Front wings rot due to road debris and salt striking them. Repair is possible, but it may be easier to bolt on a new set.

Windscreen surround A-pillars rust from the inside, with bubbling paint at the lower edge the first sign. This can be a big repair job if the rust has taken hold.

Convertible top electric drive system gears can give problems, particularly if the hood linkages are not properly cleaned and lubricated. Replacement units are quite expensive.

The underseal under the back seat can be inadequate, and rust can form here. Lifting the seat base will reveal how far it's gone.

Touring and convertible rear wheelarches are prone to rust. Repairs are sometimes complicated, and therefore expensive.

Also look under the battery tray: acid may have been spilt, which removes the paint and lets rot start.

The tailgate on Touring models relies on the drain system to avoid corrosion. Ensure it is not blocked, and make sure the seal is complete and flexible. The washer fluid tubes harden and perish, so any sign of washer fluid leaks mean the tubes will need replacing. Check the hinges for rust.

Check the jacking points for corrosion and if they are misshapen. A weak area will allow the point to bend.

Exterior trim and parts
Side mirrors are prone to aluminium corrosion, resulting in loss of paint and pitting. This can be repaired by sanding down and repainting, or by replacement.

Early cars had steel bumpers that

rot from the inside where road debris accumulates. Lifting chrome usually reveals a large rust patch.

Wipers
The windscreen wipers and rear wiper on Touring models can strip gears, preventing them moving correctly, which requires a replacement wiper motor unit. Another problem is failure of the motor switch, which results in the wiper not parking properly. The switch part can be replaced.

The wipers should operate with no squeaks or grinding noises, and park in the correct position.

Sunroof should fit level with surrounding roof. It should open and shut easily and not leak.

Sunroof

This is prone to rust around the edges. If the seals are perished, moisture may have rotted the mechanism underneath too. Check for water leaks.

Glass

The window seals perish and crack, letting in water. Moisture in the dash or on the parcel shelf could indicate failed seals. Door glass seals may have worn, which results in greater wind noise. Rear quarter light seals also leak resulting in water pooling in the side pocket.

If the rear window on convertible

models rattles or whistles at speed, the mounting washers may need adjusting, which is fairy simple.

Lights

Headlights can suffer from a milky build-up on the inside, which is difficult to shift. Also, the light mounting brackets suffer from rot, and the adjustment screws corrode so that adjustment can become impossible.

Wheels and tyres

If the car has stood for a long time, the tyres will have settled and a flat spot developed. Some people have been known to drive a car with flat spotted tyres until they are forced into an almost round shape again – unfortunately, this is very dangerous. Driving on wobbly tyres compromises handling and braking, and puts tremendous strain on the bond between cords and rubber, often resulting in unseen damage inside the tyre, which could result in a blow-out.

Tyres should be inspected all round for signs of perishing, crazing, cracks, or splits. If they show signs like these, then they need replacing. Even if the

Kerbing damage like this can be repaired. Sharp edges must be removed when fitting a new tyre.

Cracking like this means the tyre has perished. Despite there being good tread, this tyre is scrap.

crazing looks light, there could be much worse damage inside.

Tyres are generally past their best after three years, and should not be used after six, although some cheaper brands might not even last that long. Just because a tyre is still holding air doesn't mean it's in good condition. Check the four-digit date code on the side wall – as an example, '3502' would mean made in the 35th week of 2002, and a long way past its best.

Have a close look at the edge of the rim. This is where damage from bad parking near kerbs scuffs up the metal. Light scuffing will be taken in the wheel's stride, and the wheel could be refurbished, but if there are chunks taken out then they can lead to cracks forming, which slowly eat away at the metal.

Light lenses should be crystal clear. Check the mounts are sound and don't wobble. Check that all the lights work.

Gloves are needed when grabbing suspension links and checking for looseness. Hold tight and pull hard. The lower link (wishbone) rear bush is a common failure.

Seat belts

Seatbelt mountings have to cope with huge forces in a crash so that you don't have to, so any weakening here is potentially fatal. Unfortunately seatbelt mountings are also one of the top rot-spots, often due to the extra reinforcing plate spot welded in to improve localised strength, which after many years works as a moisture trap and rots in a neat outline of the plate.

Not many people realise that seat belts age too. The fabric deteriorates over time, and dirt works like an abrasive in the fibres, severely weakening them, even though they might look okay. Obviously any tears or splits mean the belt will rip apart when you need it most, Pull the belt out fully and check for any damaged threads, which will weaken the belt severely. Also check the buckle mechanism works properly.

Hub bearings, suspension joints, and steering

The traditional approach of grabbing the top of the tyre and giving a hefty pull and push to detect play is a good first step, but only shows up severely worn joints. In use, the side forces on these joints can be the equivalent of many tons, and the force you can apply by hand is a fraction of this. To maximise the usefulness of your test, the suspension has to have no load compressing the joint. Jacking up the corner and safely supporting the car will take any side loading off, then trying to wobble the wheel side-to-side as well as top and bottom is more likely to find worn joints. The most effective way of detecting the play is to have an assistant wobble the wheel whilst you hold each joint in turn, then you can feel any movement.

Whilst the wheel is raised, rotate it as fast as you can and listen for any bearing rumble. There may be a slight rubbing noise from the brakes, but any vibration or rumbling from the hub means a bearing is failing.

Interior

Often cars will contain a multitude of fungus spores and other microscopic nasties, and over the winter they may have multiplied unseen inside carpets and seats.

The smell of the interior is a useful indicator of condition. A musty smell and mould growth on the steering wheel or handbrake means it's damp.

Seats

Check the fabric for wear and tears. The outer edge of the drivers seat sees the most use, and is usually the first thing to go.

Recline the front seats and check

Damage to this driver's seat is typical. Check for tears or cracks in leather; check the seat back is secure.

for free play – the gear drive and strut can wear and make this loose.

Rock the seat back and forth to check for free play in the seat runners. A small amount is normal, but if it clonks back and forth the runners need replacing. Rot is less common on seat mountings, but it still happens. Moisture in the carpet can feed corrosion around the seat base, so lift the carpets and inspect it all thoroughly.

Head lining

There were two basic types used. Most models had a perforated vinyl sheet supported by steel rods, which are fairly durable, but do check for tears. The other sort is fabric based. A typical problem is the headlining fabric parting company with the backing. This can be repaired by removing the whole thing, taking it apart, and rebonding it with

the correct glue. Obviously this is a fair amount of work, and if you need to pay someone to do it for you, this needs to be factored into the negotiations.

Also check for marks. The fabric is quite absorbent, and removing stains can be tricky without damaging the bond.

Door locks and handles

Check all the door locks work, including the boot, using all the keys. Central-locking motors and cables seize, particularly from lack of use.

Check all the door handles work, both inside and outside. Whilst the driver's door handle will have been frequently used, the other ones may seize through lack of use, particularly the rear passenger-side door on four-door models.

Window winders

Check all the electric windows work. If the cutout has popped out, press it in and check whether all the windows work without it popping again. The door interior can be a bit damp, so mechanisms rust and the motors

corrode. Also, the side runners can move out of alignment. All this puts greater strain on the motor, slows the movement, and eventually leads to failure.

Manual winders should be smooth in operation with no tight spots.

Steering wheel

Unfortunately, an original steering wheel will have over 20 years of driver's hand sweat to contend with. Leather steering wheels will rot if not cleaned, but even soft plastic will suffer. If the car has stood for a few months there may be mould growing on this fertile base.

Non-standard steering wheels must have a proper mounting boss and be strong enough to resist bending by hand.

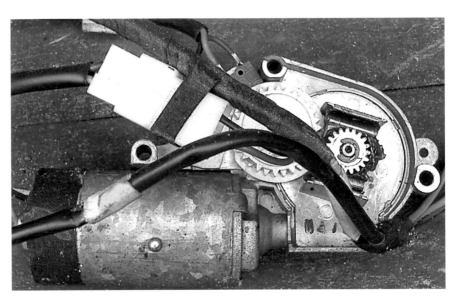

The gears on electric window winders can strip. Any grinding or jerkiness as the window rises is a cause for concern.

Check for damage all round, including the rear side where jewellery may have gradually taken out nicks.

If the steering wheel is not straight when the car is going in a straight line, this may indicate that it, or some part of the steering column or rack, has been removed and refitted in a less than professional manner. If a trackrod end has been renewed but not adjusted properly, then not only will the steering wheel be misaligned, but the tracking will be out, too.

Instrument panel

Typical faults are defective gauges and blown bulbs. When the ignition is turned on the warning lights should illuminate for a few seconds as a bulb check. The engine oil pressure warning and battery charge light should stay on until the engine starts, then go out immediately.

Run through all the switch functions to check the warning lights come on: indicators, headlights, main beam, and fog lights.

On the test run ensure all the gauges work correctly, and check that the odometer moves.

The check control unit can give false readings, but if working correctly it is usually quite useful.

Gauges

The gauges on E30s are all electric, and by now many will be starting to fail. Common problems usually turn out to be cracks on the circuit board, which can sometimes be re-soldered.

Check control

The E30 came with a small unit with

The service indicator is just a mileage counter, reset at every service by shorting two pins on the service connector, and cannot be relied upon.

an array of lights to warn about bulb and circuit failures, as well as low fluid levels. Read the handbook to understand how it works, as it can provide a useful insight. However, some units can become unreliable and show false failures.

Oil service and inspection indication

The E30 has a system that illuminates a warning light at a pre-set mileage interval when an oil change or major service is due. This is a simple system, reset by a special service tool at the dealer after servicing. It also has a countdown light, so you can tell roughly how long there is until the next service.

This system is unlikely to be of any use. Firstly, it is very easy to reset by shorting two pins on the diagnostic connector. Unscrupulous backstreet dealers may reset the timer without completing the service. Secondly, many cars are well maintained at home by enthusiasts who do not reset the system after servicing. So, you could have a well maintained car saying its service is overdue, and equally you could have a badly maintained car saying everything is fine. Best ignore it and check the fluids yourself.

Handbrake

The handbrake in disc-braked cars uses a small drum brake inside the 'hat' of the disc. Being out of sight these are

often neglected, and the mechanism can become stiff, resulting in dragging. Also the backing plate can rust and the locating pins fall out.

You shouldn't be able to pull up the handbrake lever more than eight clicks. If you can, the handbrake shoes are probably worn. Models with rear disk brakes have a manual adjuster to compensate for wear, so it could be a simple matter of adjusting it, but drum brake models have automatic adjusters, and if the lever goes too high then the shoes will need replacing.

Boot interior, spare wheel and tool kit

Boot seals perish, and water accumulates in the side sections and spare wheel well. The rear light and numberplate holes also corrode and let in moisture. Check the carpet for damp. Lift the spare wheel out and check the metal underneath. The spare should have a good usable tyre. Check for damage, and also look across the wheel and check for dents or obvious warping.

The tool kit is attached to the boot lid with a large plastic screw on Saloon and Cabriolet models, and in a bag on the left side behind a plastic panel on Touring models. It is sadly common for there to be some tool missing – the spanners had the BMW logo cast in, and some owners keep one or two as trophies. Equally sadly, the quality of the tools was not that great. If they have been used in anger they may have been damaged. If you are looking for originality then the tool kit must be complete, although individual items often come up for sale so an incomplete kit isn't final. If you are just looking for a practical car, the tool kit is of little consequence, and a reasonably priced general purpose motorist's tool kit from a high street car accessory shop makes a more practical choice.

Under-bonnet/hood

Check all the fluids. If they appear past their best, it may indicate that other

What's the general impression? Leaks and spilled fluids are signs of poor maintenance, but equally, if recently pressure-washed this may indicate an attempt to hide leaks.

The rivet area on this VIN plate clearly shows it has been removed; in this case for a respray.

Here, a cam belt is being changed. It's not a huge job for a competent mechanic, so there is no excuse for not doing it. Check the service records for evidence of the last change.

Check all the hoses for cracks and leaks, and the hose clamps for corrosion.

service items have also been missed. These things all add up to a bigger picture of the car's health.

If there is any gunge in the coolant, or 'mayonnaise' under the oil filler cap, there could be head gasket problems. Pull out the dip stick and check the level in the right range: if it is below 'Min' then it may have been neglected for some time. The oil should be a nice golden colour. If it is black, it's in desperate need of changing.

The brake fluid should be golden or clear: if it is very old and grey, the system has been severely neglected.

If the car has power steering, check the fluid level, and the same for automatic gearboxes. In both cases it should be red. Brown fluid indicates overheating and potentially a mechanical problem

The rubber intake ducts between the airbox and throttle age and crack, causing stalling or poor idling. Check all round and give them a squeeze.

Rubber generally starts cracking within ten years on a car, so look for hardening and tiny cracks appearing on coolant, oil and fuel hoses. Old coolant hoses and clips rot. Ten years is a good innings for the hoses. Prevention is better than cure, and when replacing hoses it's best to use new, good quality hose clips, because the worm drives wear and they could ping off unexpectedly.

Engine

M20 and M40 engines require regular cambelt changes. They fail without warning if left too long, so check the service history. A later style belt tensioner should be used to avoid potential seizure. Usually the water pump should be done at the same time.

Crank front pulley seals perish, resulting in oil leaks around the front lower part of the engine and potential cambelt failure.

The cylinder head on M20 engines can suffer from cracking near the water galleries, resulting in emulsified oil and water (whitish 'mayonnaise' in appearance). Heads can be repaired, but this is quite expensive, and a secondhand head may be a better route.

Head gaskets on all engines can fail, leading to emulsified coolant and oil, or loss of coolant. Gaskets are reasonably priced, and although it's a big job, replacement is reasonably straightforward for a competent mechanic.

M20 engines had a reputation for failing cylinder head bolts. The traditional hex head bolt was replaced in service with a Torx head bolt, which can be seen through the oil filler cap.

Look under the oil filler cap for signs of whitish oil contamination. Here, one of the original hex head-type bolts can be seen inside.

White vapour is normal when starting on a cold day, but once warm the exhaust should be clear. Any blue, grey or black smoke could be oil burning.

The cam front bearing seal will harden with age, allowing oil onto the belt, which weakens it. An indicator will be oil stains around the lower part of the front of the engine.

M40 engines can break cams if oil changes have been delayed.

Visco fan drives age and tend to seize. Fan noise becomes apparent at higher rpm, and the fan blades could potentially become damaged from over speeding. Also, fuel economy suffers. Failed units must be replaced.

Once the engine has warmed up, pressing the throttle fully for just one second then immediately backing off should result in the engine revving cleanly and settling back into a smooth idle. If any blue smoke is emitted, the engine may be worn and burning oil. When the engine is cold, white vapour from the exhaust is normal as water is a by-product of combustion, and as the exhaust warms up there may be a trickle of water from the tail pipe.

Another common fault is the engine coolant sensor (usually has a blue connector). They can give incorrect readings, which causes the ECU to over-fuel, resulting in poor starting, poor fuel consumption, and a loss of top-end power. This sensor was used on a great many cars, and is still readily available.

Intake and exhaust manifolds

If the intake manifold was fitted correctly, the gasket should last indefinitely, but if it has been removed at some point and refitted with a damaged gasket, there may be small leaks, which will cause the engine to run badly at idle.

The studs on the exhaust manifold corrode, then when an exhaust system is replaced they can strip their thread or snap off. Use a mirror to check they are all present and in usable condition. The manifold flange gasket will suffer if the studs have not been tightened enough. When this starts failing, there is an increased exhaust noise – a 'chuff chuff' noise – particularly at idle.

Exhaust manifolds sometimes crack. Before starting the engine, look for tell-tale black lines from escaping exhaust gas. The standard cast iron manifold should be a uniform reddish brown.

Fuel-injection system or carburettors

The most common problem is perishing of rubber seals and hoses. Examine the small fuel hoses in the engine bay and check for cracking. If an injector to fuel rail seal has failed, there will be a strong smell of fuel when the engine is running. If the fuel injector to intake manifold seal has perished it will let in air, and the engine will run badly at idle.

Carburettors are simple devices, but if the car has stood for long periods the gaskets can dry out and start leaking, and the internal parts can

This high-pressure fuel hose located under the brake servo has perished and will soon fail. The chances are that all of the other fuel hoses will be in similar condition.

become stuck with the sticky residue left over after the petrol evaporates. This renders them inoperable, but can be simply fixed by stripping them down, cleaning them, then rebuilding with new gaskets.

Exhaust system

Unless the system has been replaced in the last five years it will probably need some repairs, or possibly a replacement. Typical rust areas are the welded joints on the silencers and around the clamps at the joins. Moisture collects at the bottom of the silencer boxes, and a strip of surface rust may indicate that there is more inside.

Stainless steel exhaust systems are substantially better, but this does depend on the grade of stainless steel used, and there are some budget systems that corrode nearly as fast as the standard mild steel system. The cheaper stainless systems have welded joints that rust, which can ruin an otherwise perfectly good system.

The rear silencer has a particularly hard life, getting all the road grime and winter salt thrown at it by the back wheels. The forward face of the rear silencer usually rots out first.

Tail pipe trims, if fitted, can trap water where they clamp on to the exhaust pipe, and may rust to the point where they suddenly fall off. Check they are secure.

Gearbox, propshaft and clutch

The propshaft has large rubber couplings at each end (Guibo joints). These can fail, resulting in prop vibration and noise, followed by total failure. Also, the prop centre bearing can wear, resulting in a whining noise at speed. The surrounding rubber bushing also ages and can crack, resulting in a loud banging noise when accelerating at low speeds.

Any oil coating this area has often fallen out of the engine and been blown back during driving. This gearbox output shaft shows no signs of leakage.

Gearboxes are very reliable, but output shaft seals age and can leak oil. Generally, once mileage exceeds about 100,000 miles the gear linkages begin to wear, and gear selection becomes more sloppy. All parts are available to fix the bushes and the plastic cup that holds the ball joint, but quick shift kits are also available, which improve gear selection beyond the standard system.

Wiring

The wiring in these BMWs is generally high quality, but connectors exposed to the elements will have suffered, particularly in the engine bay. Inspect exposed connectors and check for green or white deposits.

Any additional wires that have been added should be examined carefully. If they are for auxiliary equipment make sure they are secure and have a proper fused supply, and are not simply spliced into an existing circuit. Unexplained additional wires should cause concern – they may be an attempt to bypass a serious electrical fault.

The fuse box is in the engine bay. The lid is essential to prevent corroded contacts inside. Any non-standard wires should be investigated.

Battery

If possible, take a volt meter with you. Before starting the engine check the battery voltage is above 12.0 volts – 12.6 is good, 12.2 is low but okay, and any less than 11.5 indicates a potential problem.

The battery terminals should be

The joints and edges of the boxes are typical rust-spots in exhaust systems.

The battery must be secure and the connections solid, with no corrosion.

This top swivel unit is nearly new, the rubber is smooth and not cracked, and the bearing looks new. If the rubber is peeling away from the metal it needs immediate replacement.

This rear damper bush looks fairly new. The rubber is not cracked and still bonded to the steel backing. This car also has a rear brace bar bolted to the damper towers.

free of white powdery corrosion and the earth strap connection to the body should be solid with no rust. If the cables are deteriorating, there may be green powdery deposits.

The engine should turn over swiftly at a near constant speed when you try to start it. If the speed drops significantly and repeatedly, there is a problem with either the battery or the cables.

Washer system

Operating the washer function should result in fluid instantly spraying on the windscreen. Any delay could indicate a leak.

Check the washer fluid. If left too long without adequate screenwash, it will stagnate and absolutely stink. This can pose a health risk when sprayed on the screen, as tiny particles go into the air and can be inhaled. Large plumes can also clog up the nozzles, block them, or cause a poor spray pattern, and will have to be safely flushed out.

With the ignition on but the engine not running, you should be able to hear the washer pump motor whirring. If no fluid comes out but you can still hear

the motor, it may indicate there is no fluid left, or that the pump has become detached from the motor spindle. The latter necessitates a new pump. If no sound is heard and no fluid comes out, it may indicate the pump has burned out or that the electrical connection has failed. This could be at the pump connector or the switch. If the fuse has blown, the cause of the overload should be investigated.

Suspension

The front strut top swivel bearing and bush assembly can wear and perish. If the rubber has weakened, the metal parts could knock against the bodywork and 'clonk' when going over bumps. Replacement units are reasonably priced, but fitting them involves removing the road spring.

If the rear damper mounting bushes wear out, the steel cups that hold it on can hit the bodywork. At first this causes a noise when going over bumps, then a constant rattling, and as the cups wear into the bodywork and rust takes hold, they can potentially punch through.

It is common to find that the

outer ball joint on the front control arm (wishbone) has worn, resulting in vague steering. The joint is a press fit. It could be replaced if you have the right facilities, but most people simply replace the whole arm. The most common fault is a worn rear bush – a large rubber unit at the back of the wishbone, near the footwell/bulkhead. Many people replace them with polyurethane to improve handling.

Turning the steering to full lock allows you to see the suspension properly. The lower link (wishbone) on this car has an uprated polyurethane rear bush (arrowed), which is one of the main problem areas.

movement in the bush has a minimal effect there, maintaining excellent wheel control whilst keeping the noise down. All very clever, but unfortunately this bush suffers from stress and can start breaking up, resulting in a dull rattling noise when going over rough surfaces, and a loose feeling to the steering. Replacing it is relatively easy, as it bolts to the body, but has to be pressed onto the wishbone. Often the remains of old bush will have seized on, so it may have to be cut away very carefully. If the ball

A typical rear subframe mount. The rubber bush should ensure no part of the subframe touches any part of the bracket on the body.

In common with most BMWs of that era, the lower wishbone at the front is a boomerang-shaped member with ball joints at the wheel hub and front crossmember. These should have no play in them, otherwise the handling will become vague and less predictable. The rear mounting of the lower wishbone has a very large rubber bush that isolates road noise from the car bodyshell where it is bolted on. This bush has gaps in it called 'voids,' which

allow the wishbone to move slightly when the wheels hit bumps or holes in the road. This removes shocks from the system, as well as making the ride more refined, but because the bush is located quite a long way from the wheel, any

joints are worn, the whole wishbone will have to be replaced, which can be easier than just doing the bush on its own.

Steering

Power steering systems can leak fluid. The hoses become porous with age, but also the connections can become loose, so sometimes just tightening the joint nut can help.

Seals on the rack will eventually wear. If fluid is escaping through the gaiters, a rack rebuild with new seals may be required.

Steering tie rod ball joints at the wheel end wear, particularly if the rubber boot has been damaged, resulting in vague steering. Replacement joints are reasonably cheap, and easy to fit.

This steering rack gaiter has been damaged, which lets in water and road grime, gradually eroding the joint inside.

A typical front subframe with extensive surface rust. If treated immediately, it can be saved.

This disc has light surface rust, typical of a car that has stood for a few weeks.

Subframes

The front subframe is prone to rust. Check behind each front wheel, where the subframe is bolted to the chassis rails.

The large bushes at the front of the rear subframe use large bolts to secure them to the body. As the bushes start to fail, the subframe can strike the body, causing a clonk when accelerating. Eventually a failed bush could cause the front of the subframe to drop, with severe consequences. Although bushes are cheap, they are pressed-in items so need a special tool to drift out.

Brakes

Looking through the wheel spokes you can see the brake discs. If the disc is worn, a narrow ridge will have formed at the outer edge – if this is much more than 1mm, the disc needs replacing. As the disc wears, ridges and grooves form around the surface. Gentle undulations are usually okay, but if it looks like the surface of a vinyl record then it has probably expired.

With the steering on full lock, it's possible to see the flexible brake hose.

Check for any cracks and fluid leaks.

Using the mirror and torch, you may just be able to see the brake pads. If there are only a couple of millimetres left, the pads need replacing.

Brake discs and pads are very reasonably priced, so it could be prudent to replace them on a new purchase as a matter of course.

Rear axle

The differential pan gasket can leak oil. Oil starvation or contaminated oil can cause gear wear, leading to a whining noise when accelerating, and eventually failure.

The differential mounting bushes also wear, resulting in a 'clonking' or a droning noise.

SERVICING

The E30 is a pleasantly simple car and needs a fairly low level of maintenance compared to many of its contemporaries, but that doesn't mean it should be neglected. In fact, the durability of these cars did allow some owners to skip expensive services to little obvious detriment, but left unchecked, badly maintained parts can fail without warning, with potentially disastrous results. Servicing schedules are well documented in workshop manuals and even in the owner's handbook, but here are a few things they might not cover ...

There should be no oil dripping from the front or rear. Slight oil staining from the top is due to oil mist coming out of the breather, and is usually not an issue.

Check all the right warning lights come on as soon as the ignition is turned on, then go out when the engine starts.

Beware of fake parts; always buy service items from quality suppliers. To get the maximum fun from your car, it needs to be reliable – don't cut corners on servicing.

This clutch master has a leaky top, fluid is corroding the support bracket. Also the original rubber clamp has gone.

Buying service parts

A word of warning: there is a huge number of fake service parts available. Some look identical to real parts, and even come in boxes with the correct BMW logo. Unfortunately, cheap parts are cheap because they use either cheaper materials or cheaper manufacturing methods that skip crucial aspects. A common example is a lower front wishbone, which can be an expensive part. Fake parts may use weaker metal or fail to clamp the ball joints in as firmly as needed, resulting in a sudden catastrophic failure. There are oil filters with elements that either let harmful particles through or even break up and clog oilways, cam belts that strip teeth or snap, water pumps that leak or fall apart, brake pads with friction material that falls off the backing plate – the list is endless.

The only way to be sure of the quality of the service parts is to buy from a reputable shop with a traceable supply chain. Remember, anyone can write 'Genuine BMW' on their website. Get recommendations from BMW clubs and look out for helpful specialists who have the knowledge to help you find the right part for your specific model.

Fluids

Modern fluids are far more advanced than the ones available when the E30 was launched. Engine oil in particular has come a long way, and synthetic oils last a lot longer than their mineral counterparts, which can make them more economical in the long term despite their initial expense. But it is vital to stick to the original viscosity rating – using a modern, lower viscosity oil will result in bearing damage.

Brake fluid is also much better nowadays. A good DOT5.1 will outperform the original DOT4.

The original cooling system used Glycol-based coolant. Many auto-parts stores are now promoting OTE coolant, which has a longer service life, but this does not mix with glycol-based coolants and could damage the system.

Timing belts

I always change the belt when I get a new project car, just as a precaution. The water pump is designed to be a service item on most BMW engines, so I also always change this and the idler pulley at the same time as the timing belt.

M20 engines had a revision to the timing belt idler pulley to address the bearing disintegration problem. Make sure you get the later type.

The front oil seals for the cam and crank can leak, and so whilst the front of the engine is dismantled for the belt change, it may be worth fitting new seals as a precaution. Oil leaking onto the belt will drastically reduce its life.

Window switches

The standard E30 window switches are not the best and can fail, often due to carbon building up on the contacts, getting hot, and melting the plastic support. If the windows are slow, the switches may be saved by stripping them and taking off the carbon build-up.

If none of the electric windows work there is a supply problem, check the thermal cutout switch on the dash

hasn't popped out. If it has, it may indicate a problem in the circuit.

Hoses

Rubber generally begins to crack within ten years on a car, so look for hardening and tiny cracks appearing on the coolant, oil, and fuel hoses. I prefer to replace them as a matter of course on any new project – they are a lot cheaper to replace than a seized engine!

Intake ducts

Temporary repairs can be made with self-amalgamating rubber tape (really useful stuff), but replacement parts are relatively cheap, so worth fitting if there is any damage.

Door locks

If the key won't turn, do not force it. Instead, squirt in some WD40 and leave it for an hour or so, then try gently wiggling the key until it frees.

RECOMMISSIONING

Chances are you will lay up your E30 over winter, or maybe you are looking at buying a car that has stood for a year or so. Here is a list of thing to look out for after it's been off the road.

There are two main problems: fluids degrade, and, as with all of us, inactive joints can seize up. So for these reasons never just hop in the car and try firing it up. Instead, start by giving it a thorough inspection, not least for any evidence of infestation my mice or insects, which can wreak havoc when they make nests out of wiring or hoses. Look under the car for little piles of gnawed-through cable or rubber, and look for tell-tale collections of nut shells, too. If there is evidence, start stripping back the car in that area until the culprit is found and the damage fixed.

Also check every rubber part. Rubber perishes over time even if unused, so look for small cracks, which indicate it has hardened and needs replacing. Tyres rarely last more than six years, and even coolant hoses struggle to last more than ten years. It is far better to replace a cheap hose than to risk it, and potentially have to fix an overheated or seized engine.

Pull off the wheels and have a good look. Check the brake hoses, suspension joints, brake pads/shoes, and wheel bearing. Corrosion and fatigue can lurk in all sorts of nooks and crannies, and only an intensive search will avoid you finding out about it later, the hard way.

Battery

Hopefully, the battery was removed prior to the car being laid up, and put on a trickle charger. If not, it will have discharged. Assess its electrolyte condition, and if it is still serviceable put it on charge to get it up to full strength. Depending on its condition this may take up to a day.

For 12v batteries the open circuit voltage at the terminals should be above 12.5 volts when charged; 11.5 is discharged and will struggle to start an old engine, but if it's heavily discharged it may never give reliable service, and replacement is the only option. If it's at 7v or lower, it's probably broken.

Before refitting the battery, clean the terminals and connectors, and when reconnected coat them in a suitable grease. Even a thin layer of corrosion will reduce starting ability.

Coolant (antifreeze)

The stuff you add to the water does a number of important jobs, one of which is inhibit corrosion. Using the right concentration is vital, but over time it becomes acidic and can eat away at the engine from the inside. Most types of coolant should last about three years, but it is wise to replace it every year on a classic to minimise degradation.

While the coolant is out, give the rad and engine a quick flush through with a garden hose, to remove any loose debris that has settled. E30 engines have alloy heads on iron blocks, which can react if the coolant has insufficient corrosion inhibitor in. Water can leach the silicon from the aluminium alloy,

resulting in blobs of silicone jelly forming and a weakening of the alloy. Tap water has air dissolved in it, which can react with the alloy to produce white powdery aluminium oxide. Typically, this forms under the top hose on the thermostat housing, slowly eating away at the metal until it leaks or suddenly blows off the top hose when the engine gets hot. So it's worth inspecting every joint where a rubber hose goes on to a metal part. If the corrosion is light, it may be scraped off and the surface smoothed to get a good seal. In extreme cases, the metal part may have to be replaced.

Tyres/tires

Hopefully, the car will have been on stands over the winter, otherwise the tyres will have settled and flat spots developed. Some people have been known to drive a car with flat-spotted tyres until they are forced into an almost round shape again – unfortunately, this is very dangerous. Driving on wobbly tyres compromises handling and braking, and puts tremendous strain on the bond between cords and rubber, often resulting in unseen damage inside the tyre, which could cause a blow-out.

Tyres should be inspected all round for signs of perishing, crazing, cracks,

The steering should feel light and accurate once on the move. This is one of the E30's strongest features.

or splits, whereupon replacement will be necessary. If they show signs like these, then they need replacing. Even if the crazing looks light, there could be much worse damage inside.

Tyres are generally past their best after three years, and should usually not be used after six, although some cheaper brands might not even last that long. Just because a tyre is still holding air doesn't mean it's in good condition.

Finally, set the correct tyre pressures before heading out.

Brakes

Brakes can bind when the car has been stood for long periods. The friction material can bond to the metalwork, whether drums or discs. This can usually be freed off, but if there is any damage to the friction material it must be replaced. The drum or disc may have light corrosion. If it's only a light dusting, a quick sanding will remove it, but deep pitting will need to be fixed by resurfacing or replacing. Never try to free brakes or remove rust by driving – first, you should never take a car with faulty brakes on the road; second, this method may rip the friction surface or embed rust particles in it and reduce its efficiency. You have to do it the hard way by stripping them.

Sometimes hydraulic brakes can bind on for a different reason; the small

E30 performance is good even by modern standards. This 325i entertains on a test track.

head of pressure due to the master cylinder being higher than the wheels can cause the pistons to very slowly creep out. If this has occurred, the pistons need to be prised back enough so that the seals can retract the piston normally.

Hopefully the car was stored with the handbrake off, otherwise it may well bind as described before. Again, strip-down is the best cure.

Now is the perfect time to replace the brake fluid. It will have had all winter to absorb moisture, so flush it all away. Silicone fluid doesn't absorb water, but moisture still gets trapped in the system, so flushing it through will reduce that danger.

When inspecting the brake material, have a very close look at where the friction material is bonded to its backing. This bond can weaken over time and crack. I have seen brake pads where the whole of the friction material has come away from the backing and been spat out of the calliper during an emergency stop. Even though the pads had plenty of depth to them they had in fact perished.

Oil

Oil absorbs moisture, and things like engine blocks, gear casings, and even differential housings can accumulate a lot of condensation as the cold winter days go by, so it's worth at least inspecting the oil – drain a little out of the bottom and check for water where possible – but the best option is to change it completely.

One word of caution, though: the oil in the engine may have drained out of the pick-up tube and oil pump, so it may be prudent to run the engine before changing the oil, or at least crank it over with the plugs out until the oil pressure warning light goes out, so the pump isn't sucking on air. Also, never remove the oil filter when the sump is drained; at least with a loaded filter there is some oil in the system, rather than air. You will also benefit from priming the new oil filter with fresh oil before fitting.

After the test drive, look through the front grille, above and below the bumper, checking for any coolant or oil leaks.

Electrics

The vibration from running a car seems to keep connectors working much better than if the car were laid up. Some connectors can be stirred back to life with a little wiggle, and some switches may need a few operations to clean their contacts. So as soon as the car is running, go through each electrical system, use it a few times, and check all is well. Replace any suspect connections.

Obviously jiggling connectors is not a long-term solution, and although this is fine for just getting something working, eventually the connector will have to be cleaned up or replaced.

Mechanicals

Grease and oils will have been squeezed out of any joint which has had load on it, so spin the wheels before taking the car off the stands.

Bounce the corners of the car and

A Cabriolet model's roof should latch in securely with no gaps. Look for water marks on the inside.

Locks can become stiff, particularly if the car has remote locking. Check the key works in all locks.

listen for creaking, which may indicate a bush is rotating in its housing and will need replacing.

Screen/windshield wash

Flush the bottle with a high concentration of quality screen wash. Old water may have become stagnant and smelly. It can also develop growths that can clog the washer jets, so a good flush through, first with the tubes removed from the jets, then with them reconnected, will set it up for the summer.

Bodywork

The chances are that waxes or oils will have been applied to prevent corrosion before laying up the car. Now's the time to remove them. Inspect for damage and give it a good clean followed by waxing to seal everything up. Don't forget to clean the windows and mirrors.

Interior

Often cars will contain a multitude of fungus spores and other microscopic nasties, and over the winter they may have grown unseen inside carpets and seats, so give it all a good clean and a vacuuming. Clean and feed any leather before putting it under load. And don't forget to clean the inside of the windows, too.

Engine

Check the belts are tensioned and have not deteriorated. Check and lubricate the throttle, and make sure it returns shut smoothly. The oil will have drained off every surface, including cam lobes, and the piston rings may have started to cold weld onto the bores, so the first fire-up is critical.

Some say it's best to raise the oil pressure by turning the engine over with the spark plugs out. Unfortunately, if it turns over slowly it may damage the cam lobes, so make sure the battery is fully charged and all the connections are clean. A drop of oil added to the cylinder – hopefully before it was laid

up, but in any case when you are about to turn it over – will help the engine turn over swiftly. In any case, if the oil pressure does not come up within a few seconds, stop and investigate the cause.

When the engine is first run, it is essential that it starts quickly, so make sure everything is ready; ensure there is plenty of fresh fuel in the tank. Modern fuels form heavy deposits, much more so than fuels of old, which can cause carburettors and injectors to stick, so if fresh fuel can be brought through to the engine then so much the better.

Check the plugs, distributor cap and rotor arm have not corroded or tarnished – clean them if needed. Ensure all the connections are sound. When everything is cued up and ready, start it, and as soon as the oil pressure light goes out raise the revs to about 2000rpm to minimise cam loading, leave it there for a few seconds whilst the oil is pumped round, then return to idle. Once it is running smoothly, inspect it for leaks. If all is well, allow it to warm up, constantly checking for funny noises and leaks.

Removing rust from small parts

Iron oxide (rust) can be turned back into metal by removing the oxygen in a strong acid. This may sound drastic, but cheap malt vinegar does the trick. I use an economy brand from the local supermarket and leave small rusted parts to soak for a few days in a bucket. When they're done, there is usually some gunge left on the surface that can be scrubbed off with an old toothbrush. I then give the parts a rinse and coat them in WD40 to clean off the vinegar and residue.

Chapter 4
Modification

INTRODUCTION

If you are keen on modifying cars, I bet you turned to this chapter first. If so, well done, but before ripping into your E30 there is something to think about. The E30 is already a good car, so ask yourself: why are you modifying it? The answer will generally fall into one of the following categories:

1. The car is faulty or tired, and you fancy pepping it up at the same time as fixing it. In which case stay focused on only fixing the things that actually need fixing. Don't get sidetracked. Modifying can be addictive, and many 'unfinished projects' start this way.

2. You are going to race it. In which case start by reading the race regulations, then read them again until you really understand them. If you make a non-regulation modification, you are not going racing.

3. There is some aspect that annoys you and you want to change it, possibly the power or handling. In which case write down exactly what annoys you, make it clear, and then focus clearly on modifications that will directly

It is amazing how little BMW modified its works M3 Touring Car to make a hugely competitive race car. (Courtesy BMW)

tackle this problem. Again, it is easy to get sidetracked.

4. Because you want to. In which case there are no rules, it also means

38

A side-by-side comparison of the road M3 and the race M3. Success came from building on the E30's strengths, and re-engineering only where needed. (Courtesy BMW)

Big modifications require a lot of workshop space, and plenty of storage, too.

When thinking about tuning the engine, consider the whole car: cooling, intake, exhaust, fuel systems, and even the electrical system: all have a part to play.

the car will never be 'finished,' there will always be the next modification. It is easy for this sort of project to take over your life. If you are single and want to stay that way, carry on. Everyone else should tread carefully.

Whatever the reason, the same basic rules apply:

1. Understand the budget and work within it.

2. Understand your ability and work within it – call professionals when needed.

3. Understand your time constraints – be realistic and plan accordingly.

4. Understand the space needed. When stripping a car for restoration or modification, it always seems to need a floor space three times bigger than the car. I find jobs work best when there is ample storage space and plenty of room around the car to do the work comfortably.

Don't just keep your plan in your head — write it down and remember to reread it regularly throughout the project.

The theory of cheap motorsport

Motorsport at any level is hugely enthralling, but the costs are prohibitive for the vast majority of enthusiasts. There are, however, a few ways round

this, and it is possible to do a day's competition for less than the cost of a full tank of fuel.

The fastest cars in drag racing accelerate from 0 to 100mph in 0.8 of a second, and exceed 330mph in quarter of a mile, but they will spend 500 quid on fuel for each run, followed by replacing most of the 50 grand engine. By comparison, clubs like the Slow Car Club take bangers usually costing less than 500 quid up the track at Santa Pod on Run What Ya Brung days, and entry costs about 35 quid for a whole day of driving flat out. It doesn't matter how fast the car is, because after the first few runs you start trying to beat your personal best time. It is highly addictive, and lots of fun.

If you have ever fancied rally driving, but haven't got a rally car, and baulk at the £300 entry fee for even the smallest of events, drop down a few gears and look at production car trials. As the name suggests the cars are standard, and there are classes for different engine sizes and engine/drive configurations. 4x4s are banned, so not one for the 325ix.

The setup is simple: take a muddy hill with a few obstacles, mark out a challenging twisty course, and see how far you can drive a car up the track before getting stuck. About the only modification you can make to the car is dropping the tyre pressures and taking the front chin spoiler off. The tracks are divided into ten sections, and you

get penalty points depending on how badly you do. If you manage to get all the way up, you have no penalties and it's a clear run. The skill required is remarkable, and it is easy to get utterly immersed in the task of coaxing your banger that extra few inches up the track – it's just as addictive as high-speed track racing, and highly recommended.

Another variant on the rally theme is the twelve car event. This is a navigational event run on public roads, so speeds are modest. A route is issued to the drivers at the start line, and timekeepers are stationed at the end of each section. The skill is the teamwork between navigator and driver, to ensure the best route is taken and speed optimised to make sure the car arrives at precisely the right time. It's very competitive, requiring self control as much as car control – going too fast is as bad as too slow. Here a well-maintained standard E30 really shines.

You have probably seen footage of cars being expertly drifted round a very tight course laid out with cones, usually in a car park. This is autotesting, and is a measure of drivers skill against the clock whilst negotiating hairpin bends, reverse parking, and tight slaloms. You'll need good tyres to get the best out of the car, but for road car classes that's about the only thing you can change. Precision and pace are needed in bucket loads. You think you can handle a car? This will make you think again!

The E30 has a strong following. As soon as you start on your project, you are sure to get 'help' from your friends. Make sure anyone helping knows exactly what you need them to do to get the results you want.

This is what it's all about – early morning at a race track with your project car all ready. Nothing beats the feeling.

But if driving flat out round corners is high on your list of needs, consider hillclimb or sprints. These are usually on racetracks and do require a race licence, so the costs start mounting, but it does mean you can drive at high speeds on real circuits. The idea is simple – to get from the start line to the finish line as fast as possible, and it's wonderful to watch as there is often old F1 machinery operating in the upper classes. If you are wondering what the difference is, a hillclimb is uphill and a sprint is on the flat, more or less. Again, a well-maintained standard E30 can work very well, but there are also classes for modified cars where the E30's light weight and tunability can work very well, too.

There is a surprising wealth of cheap motorsport opportunities in the UK. If you are handy with the spanners, there is grass track (sprint races in a field), stage rallying, economy runs (more fun than you might think), and even real circuit racing can be done on a budget of less than £3000.

The trackday

If you just want to drive flat out and are not so interested in competing against other drivers, the trackday is for you.

Track days punish cars, running flat out for long periods, so it is vital to spend a bit of time making things like the cooling system, engine mounts, and fuel system etc work properly. Remember to fully service the engine and use the best quality oil. Don't worry about tuning the engine for more power: you are not in a race, and it will just put more strain on it.

As ever, tyre choice is critical, but in a very different way to a racing car. A fun track car needs durable tyres that give consistent handling and let you play all day; after all, a bit of drifting just adds to the fun, and it is easier to learn your track craft with tyres that break away controllably, rather than race tyres that will grip more but break away abruptly. Some people have had good results buying part-worn performance road tyres, but there are pitfalls here, and the tyres must be inspected by an expert.

Next on the list are the brakes. Heavy, repeated braking builds ferocious heat, so race brake fluid and pads will prevent catastrophic fade. On a low budget, use new standard discs, but avoid fakes. Uprated pads such as EBC Green Stuff can add bite, but a good prevention against fade is to use race brake fluid such as Motul RBF600.

Stripping the interior is always a favourite. It is amazing how little difference this usually makes to performance, but lowering weight does reduce the strain on the car a bit, and it makes the car feel more like a racing car. Just remember to keep useful things like door handles and mirrors, and make sure there are no sharp edges that could cut you in an accident.

For tight budgets you are unlikely to get a lowered suspension kit worth having, but fitting a pair of stiffer front dampers will make a big difference. Secondhand dampers may be worn, so are best avoided, although adjustable ones can sometimes be wound up to compensate.

If you go to any trackday, you will notice that by lunchtime a fair number of cars will have retired with silly faults. Spend as much time and money as you can checking and replacing worn parts to make the car as reliable as possible. A broken car is no fun at all.

ENGINE INTRODUCTION

When tuning any engine, there are some basic principles that need to be

The M Power philosophy is very well worth noting. It built on the existing strengths and made new parts only where needed. (Courtesy BMW)

understood. Small changes make small gains, and whilst any engine will have compromises for production, cost, emission, and economy, changing only one aspect of an engine will never transform it. All the E30 engines are reasonably well-tuned road engines as standard, so just changing the air filter or rear silencer will not make much improvement in performance.

For tuning purposes there are two different paths depending on what you are trying to achieve: if it is a race engine, you are going for the maximum average power for the whole rev range used between gear shifts, but if the engine is for a road or trackday car, it is best tuned to give you the most enjoyment. This doesn't mean absolute on-the-limit power, but it does need to suit your driving style. A fun engine must also sound right, and even the way it looks can be important.

Using race parts on a road engine can often be a mistake. As ever, before tuning an engine it is vital to ensure it is in good condition and properly set up. There is no point sticking a performance cam in if the valves are covered in hard carbon deposits. Ideally the engine would be stripped and cleaned before starting, ensuring the combustion chamber has no carbon deposits that will cause knocking, and making sure the crank bearings are okay, the ring gaps within tolerance, etc. It depends how far you want to go. If you just want

Cams form the heart of the engine, but are so often badly fitted. This one had no cam lube and was not run-in, resulting in tip wear and loss of performance.

a mild improvement to make the car feel a little more lively, maybe a full service is all it needs, but if you are looking to double the output, every part should be examined and replaced if needed.

The engine oil is another important factor. Using the right type that can cope with the extremes of temperature and pressure is vital – use the wrong type, and friction and hydrodynamic drag increase will lead to increased wear and reduced power. Race oils are expensive and may not work so well at very low temperatures, but will resist the destructive forces and temperatures experienced in a race, so as ever it is a matter of using the right thing for the job.

The same logic applies to the coolant too. For very high-power engines such as a 400bhp turbo M20, it may help to reduce the glycol content and put in a bottle of 'water wetter' which increases heat transfer at the expense of very low temperature protection.

Even gaskets and seals should be considered as part of a high-performance engine. Talk to any successful race engine builder and they will tell you that the secret is in the details.

For best tuning results, the most important thing is to consider the exhaust, intake, cams, and head as a part of the whole system, from air filter to tail pipe. Things like the air filter or exhaust are not an isolated subsystem that can be altered on its own without affecting everything else.

When the exhaust valve opens, you need the waste gases to leave the chamber as swiftly as possible: the lower the pressure in the exhaust port at that moment, the better. Once it gets going, its momentum will help it keep going, even if the pressure in the port rises a little bit. In fact, we can use this to help with the intake too. If you get the exhaust gas moving fast enough you can generate enough momentum such that it will actually drag in charge as soon as the intake valve opens, but if you overdo it the intake charge gets dragged straight through to the exhaust with hilarious consequences (pop, bang, bang, kaboom). This happens when both intake and exhaust valves are open at the same time, at the end of the exhaust stroke and the beginning of the intake stroke, and is called overlap. This timing is a crucial part of cam designs, as we shall see later.

The way to increase the exhaust gas speed is to use a smallish port, but this limits the maximum flow, so it's all a bit of a balancing act. If you have a big port, the exhaust can start to flow more easily, but the speed will be lower so it can slow down easily too, or even reverse if the conditions are right, which is why classic race engines don't idle smoothly.

To improve mid-range torque, increase port velocity by reducing port size, as with the BMW Eta heads. However, this will cause a restriction at higher speeds and so lower peak power. It's a balancing act all the way through.

All the above ignores the effects of pressure waves bouncing around, which can be significant. Every time the exhaust or intake valve opens or shuts, there is a change in port pressure. This

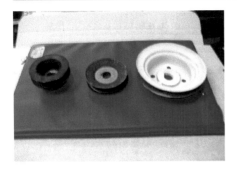

The secret of very high power is rpm, but don't forget to resize the pulleys to prevent the alternator and water pump over-speeding. Details like this are vital for reliability.

The whole system must be considered, from intake to exhaust. Every part influences how the gas flows. This M3 has an intake, throttle bodies, ports, valves, combustion chamber, pistons, and exhaust that all work together.

wave travels down the exhaust or intake system doing all sorts of interesting and complicated things, but a gross over simplification can be used for practical purposes: every time the pulse comes out of a pipe (say at a manifold junction or into a silencer), a negative wave travels back up the pipe to the valve. Pulse tuning involves making the intake and exhaust manifolds the right length so that a negative pressure arrives at the exhaust and a positive pressure arrives at the intake valve just as it opens.

Cams are usually described by their duration – that is, the total amount of degrees in a cycle during which a valve is open. The standard M20 cam opens the intake valve 11 degrees before top dead centre (BTDC), and closes again at 47 degrees after bottom dead centre (ABDC), giving a total duration of 238 degrees. Similarly, the exhaust opens 51 degrees BBDC and closes 7 degrees ATDC which also gives 238 degrees duration. This, then, would be referred to as a 238 cam. Performance cams open the valves for longer, have more overlap when intake and exhaust valves are open at the same time, and usually have more lift, too.

As a rough guide, a cam of about 270 degrees would add a touch of sportiness to a road car, a 290 would be for a fast road or trackday car, and race

engines may take anything up to 310 degrees, although this will not idle at all well, and also requires tuned intake and exhausts, as well as head work, to work properly.

When fitting a new cam, it is vital to use new followers and sticky cam lube so that the very thin, hardened surfaces of the cam lobes and followers are not ripped up due to lack of oil when first started. This massively extends the life of the cam, and is more important on higher lift cams that force the valve open faster because they put higher loadings on the lobes. The first time an engine is run after a new cam install, assuming there are no faults, it is wise to run at about 2000rpm for a few minutes. Higher speeds can damage the lobes, but lower speeds give the oil enough time to be expelled, and also increases initial wear, so a nice mid-speed rpm is best for the first few minutes.

After about 2000 miles most people check and adjust the valve clearance again, as the valves will have worn very slightly and settled in. In fact, one of the key factors in performance tuning is valve clearance, which is tragically often overlooked, and yet very easy to adjust on E30 engines. From a racing point of view I prefer to check

the clearances when the engine is fully hot, because this is when they matter most, but this involves difficulties due to cooling of the head and the danger of burnt fingers, so for practical reasons the clearances are usually set when cold. One thing to remember is that when dealing with very small tolerances, the oil film on the feeler gauge will make a small difference. The trick is to be consistent, so I coat the feeler in engine oil before the first measurement.

Compression ratio should be considered in conjunction with cam choice. A high ratio can yield more power, but increases knock tendency – 9.75:1 is usually about the upper limit for a road car engine. But wilder cams admit less air at mid speeds and so the actual cylinder pressures can be lower than on a stock engine, reducing knock tendency. This allows an increase in compression ratio. For instance, a 300 degree cam could potentially run nicely with a compression ratio of about 10.5:1.

High revving race engines might run compression ratios of over 12:1.

Turbocharging
Undoubtedly this is the most effective way of getting more air into an engine. There are many turbo M20 engines about that make over 400bhp, but force feeding an engine that was never designed for it does bring some challenges. See section 6 to find out more.

Carburettors
The original carburettor on the 316 is not a performance option, but some people like carbs, and a set of three dual choke sidedraught carbs on stubby manifolds sounds epic. Of course, you could get the same effect by using throttle bodies and injection. This gives the engine a greater operating range, and the lack of venturi chokes improves power.

Carbs can be an attractive option if you enjoy the simplicity of a purely mechanical fuelling system. However, injection systems are so prolific that their relative cheapness and better fuel control can make them a far better performance tuning option.

4-CYLINDER ENGINE TUNING

The 4-cylinder E30 engines have the advantage of lightness compared to the 6-cylinder engines. This makes the car feel more lively round tight corners, and is arguably a better choice for racing.

Indeed, all the E30 4-cylinder engines have a very strong iron block bottom end, and can be made to work very well at remarkably high rpm, or even with a turbo or supercharger, with the potential to exceed the performance of a naturally aspirated 6-cylinder engine by quite a large margin.

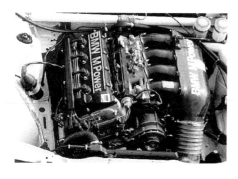

This is an M3 Touring Car. Note the larger intake system with its cold air feed, and the radiator size. With fast airflow, even 370bhp doesn't need a massive cooler. (Courtesy BMW)

M10

Initially the E30 was offered with the old 4-cylinder M10 engine in 1.8-litre form, with carburettors on the 316 and injection on the 318i. These are very tough old engines that have been used since 1961. The old iron lump that powered the 1500 and 2002 BMWs also went into the E21 3 Series of the 70s. As a naturally aspirated engine, it began its career putting out less than 70bhp, but people soon began racing BMWs in Touring Cars and other great race series, and its capability to rev like

There's a reason they chose the M10 as the base for the M3: it's one of the toughest small engines on the planet. The standard S14 is a very well tuned engine already; significant improvements can be pricey. (Courtesy BMW)

hell quickly won it medals, the mighty 1.5 managing a very impressive 300bhp when ally twin-cam heads were made for it.

By using a very big KKK turbo and a Bahr intercooler (very slightly bigger than the radiator), it is essentially this version that became the legendary F1 engine. The short stroke (60mm in an 89.2mm bore) let the engine rev reliably to nearly 12,000rpm, and produced about 1500bhp in qualifying trim (where the engine would last for two or three laps) or about 1200bhp in race trim!

Later, the iconic M3 used that same old iron block M10 as the base for the 238bhp S14 engine, this time with the M division's favourite 4-valve head design and twin-cams, which used a similar design to the M88 6-cylinder engines.

Elsewhere in the BMW range, the M10 was available as a 2.0-litre engine, 2002, 320/4 or 520/4. The M10B20 can make a nice bolt-in upgrade to a

tired 1.8, and makes about 130bhp as standard.

The M10's relation to the M3 S14 engine means parts are available to take it up to 2.4 litres.

Tuning the standard M10 revolves around revs, a wild cam, and helping the head flow well.

If you like carbs, the Weber 32/36 DGV is a good bolt-on option to replace the standard Solex, but of course, nothing looks or sounds quite the same as a set of sidedraught DCOE carbs, ranging from 40 DCOE with 34mm venturis for mildly tuned road cars, up to 45s for race motors.

Compression ratio should be considered in conjunction with cam choice. For instance, a Schrick 304 cam could potentially run nicely with a compression ratio of about 10.5:1, but very high revving race engines might run compression ratios over 12:1.

The standard heads respond very well to sporty cams in the 280 to 295 range. 150bhp is potentially available with a good intake system and standard exhaust.

Full race engines run cams up to 336 degrees, with a power band that starts at 5000rpm and extends to around 9000rpm, giving a potential of around 220bhp.

For high powers, the standard fuel-injection system struggles, as the airflow meter can be restrictive when increasing power by more than about 10%. Some companies offer modifications to the ECU to run without an airflow meter, but another option is to fit a mappable ECU system, preferably allowing mapped ignition too, to make the best use of the whole rev range.

As the block is so strong, the M10 takes forced induction very well. If you have the money, 500bhp is possible at very high rpm and boost.

To keep it all together at high rpm, the whole bottom end needs to be properly balanced – crank, rods, pistons, and pulley, as well as the flywheel and clutch. Also, pay attention to the rocker arms, which can fatigue due to casting roughness creating stress risers. Race engines should have the underside of the rockers (which is in tension) smoothed.

M40

The M10 replacement was the M40, still with a 2-valve head design to keep low and mid range torque. It has a good strong bottom end in an iron block, but the heads can sometimes be prone to cracking and cam wear.

The usual tuning rules apply, and performance cams are available, but it is relatively difficult and expensive to make large gains on this engine compared to other E30 engines. It is usually far easier to start with the twin-cam M42, usually sourced from an E36, and use either the whole engine or just the head.

The M40 is, sadly, an unloved engine. Large gains might be more economically achieved with a different type of engine, but it can still be a good budget choice and make a fun track car.

M42

This was a 4-valve head design based on the M40 block. It saw service in the 318is and continued into the E36 3 Series cars.

With a slightly larger throttle body and ECU remap, 150bhp is achievable. A balanced bottom end, cams with a duration of 280 to 290 degrees, a good intake and exhaust can produce over 200bhp.

Good servicing is vital. The distributor, cam belt, idler, and water pump should be replaced on a new project as a matter of course.

Although the head has good power potential, it is fairly delicate, so it's vital to ensure it never overheats. Some engines had a water pump with a plastic impeller that can fail suddenly – far better to use the steel impeller version. When building a performance M42, it is wise to replace the cam chains, tensioners, and sprockets, which can wear quite rapidly.

M3 S14

The S14 came in two displacements: initially as a 2.3, then in the Evo 3 as a 2.5. So for earlier cars there is the option of upgrading to the later engine spec. The S14 is already a very well tuned engine – any further increase in power will be at the expense of some low-speed torque, which can adversely affect drivability. However, the S14 was used very successfully in competition, so there is a wealth of tuning parts available, for a price. The maximum capacity increase is to about 2.7 litres, but the main gains come from increased revs coupled with more aggressive cams. As ever, rebuilding and fully balancing the bottom end is essential for large gains.

BMW motorsport DTM racing M3s used larger airboxes and throttles. Coupled with race cams and a fantastic tubular exhaust manifold, these produced about 370bhp using the 2.5

Throttle bodies are an **M Power** favourite, but can be a little tricky to set up and can result in less torque at low rpm. If done well, however, they help produce higher power and sound awesome. (Courtesy BMW)

engine, but to build one of these would cost more than the price of a perfect standard M3 car!

6-CYLINDER ENGINE TUNING
M20 engines

The standard 6-cylinder E30 engine is a very solid iron block lump with good tuning potential.

The original M20B20 in 1977 (E21) had relatively narrow ports to increase port velocity and improve low speed torque with carburettors. These heads are known as #1264200, or '200.'

With the introduction of the E30 and L Jetronic fuel-injection system, the 2.0 had enlarged ports in the #1277731 or '731' head, and received larger valves in 1987, when the injection system switched to Motronic.

The 2.5 was designed with performance in mind from the start, so had the larger valves and ports in the #1705885 or '885' head casting. This also had a different piston design and a higher volume combustion chamber to reduce knock, so plonking one on a 320 will lower the compression ratio.

With over 200bhp easily achievable, the 325i makes a very popular budget racer or trackday toy.

The 325i block came in two flavours. The early E30 2.5-litre engine had a higher compression ratio of 9.75:1 and was known as '84 6E,' but after 1988 the compression was dropped to 8.8:1 and the engine was known as '84 6K,' the 'K' indicating exhaust catalyst.

The block on the 325ix 4WD has a significantly different design for the oilways, due to the front half-shaft passing through the sump. This makes it difficult to replace with any of the other M20 blocks.

The 2.7 Eta engine

A lot of negative comments surround this engine, which is deeply unfair because it is very well designed. The idea was to produce an engine with very high economy and similar real world performance to the 325i. BMW attained very high port velocities by using the small port '200' head (using only five of the normal seven cam bearings and softer valve springs to further reduce friction losses), minimal cam overlap, and a small throttle to ensure the low speed torque was very high. With 84mm (3.3in) bore and a longer 81mm (3.2in) stroke for a displacement of 2693cc, the result is 'only' 121bhp, but 172lb-ft and a wide range of usable torque, so most ordinary drivers would be able to drive just as fast in real world conditions as they would in a 325i – the difference would be noticed only when driving fast. In its final year of production it was fitted with 885 heads, with pistons and modified intakes to match.

Interestingly, the 2.7 block was used by Alpina to make its 327i, with the long stroke crank from the diesel M21, 325i heads, and Alpina's own cams. BMW South Africa also used the 2.7 with the 885 heads to replace its 333, initially with an identical 197bhp, but later upped to 210bhp, which shows this engine's potential.

325e (Eta) cars are fairly rare, so most conversion engines are sourced from the 525e instead, but with the 325i sump, cylinder head, pistons, and ancillaries fitted. With a good performance road cam (something like a 270) this combination has been shown to produce around 225bhp with a good spread of torque.

Just putting an 885 325i head on a standard Eta block results in a lower compression ratio of about 8.3:1. Whilst this is pretty poor for a naturally aspirated engine, it is quite good for a turbo or supercharged engine. Such setups have been known to make 400bhp.

The Eta crank is supposedly a strong item and good for over 7500rpm.

The magnificent M20, this one from an early 325i. Again, the iron block is no lightweight, but its strength means that high power is attainable without too much expense.

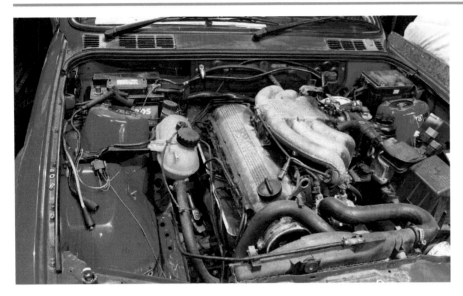

The M20 offers a large number of tuning options. Using standard parts, capacities of 2.0, 2.3. 2.5 and 2.7 can be had.

The first step in tuning is the right service parts. A change of sparkplug, the right oil, and decent coolant all have a part to play.

The Eta engines had a low rev limit of 4750rpm, but this was because the relatively light valve springs would start floating above 5000, and anyway, the narrow ports wouldn't flow much air at higher speeds. It is possible to swap in the turbo-diesel M21 crank, which has the same dimensions as the Eta crank, but is forged rather than cast for even greater strength.

Another interesting idea is to use the crank from a different BMW engine in the M20 block. An M52, S50US, S52US, or M54 forged crank requires minimal modification – just a spacer to accept the front crank oil seal, and a different crank pulley bolt, although there can be clearance problems that may require a small amount of adjustment.

The 84mm stroke crank of an M52 with the 130mm con rods from the 320/323/early 325E, and 885 325i cylinder head and pistons, gives a 2.8-litre engine with a compression ratio of 9.7:1 the potential for about 230bhp.

The largest M20 conversion I have heard of is 3.1 litres, using the 89.6mm stroke crank from a S52US or M54B30 and the maximum re-bore size of 86mm.

Going beyond 86mm bore is generally considered risky as there is very little metal left. The M20 bore spacing is 91mm, so this only leaves 5mm between cylinders, and most of that is water!

Porting and head work

If the starting point is the 885 head, BMW has pretty much done all the work already. It's difficult to get any big improvements – even bigger valves would be shrouded by the cylinder walls. Gains can be made, but they are small for the price, so unless you are constrained by your race regulations, you may be better off spending the money on other modifications.

The M20 responds well to having the exhaust valve clearance increased by two thousandths of an inch. This appears to give a more stable idle and reduce valve rattle.

Make sure the oil spray bar is clear – sludge can block it, and then it's just a matter of time before oil starvation wrecks the cam lobes. Remove it and clean with carb cleaner or similar.

The BMW motorsport cam gear has been fitted to M20 engines. It retards the exhaust camshaft of the

'88-'91 M3 and '88-'89 M5 and M6. This allows for better exhaust scavenging, which in turn gives a moderate +11lb-ft torque increase, and aids every day drivability.

Sparkplugs in a race application have to cope with high heat levels for longer, so should be changed for ones of a higher heat grade. In this case we will go for NGK BPR6ES, which allegedly give a few more bhp.

One thing that is often overlooked is oil. This not only dictates the reliability of the engine in extreme conditions, but also has a significant effect on power losses due to drag, friction, and windage as the spinning crank whacks into blobs of flying oil. Using the right grade is essential, as are additives that can cope with extended high temperatures

Turbo or supercharging

The M20 is a tough old block, and I have heard tales of essentially standard engines coping with a 12psi boost. The weakest links are arguably the cylinder head bolts and head gasket. Swapping for race-style head studs, or just good quality high-tensile head bolts and a good quality new head gasket, should be considered the minimum upgrade for a pressure-charged engine. Any engine that is being built for substantially more power should be compression and leak checked, then fully stripped and all new

The M20 is sensitive to ignition components. Buy genuine parts. This engine is about to have the engine-driven fan removed, freeing up a little power and helping with access to the front of the engine.

It's amazing how many tuned engines have badly set throttles. Always adjust the cable to get full throttle movement. Race cars require two throttle return springs for safety.

correctly mapped. Extreme tuners have claimed 1000bhp for exotic and expensive builds. The great thing about a boosted engine is that you have a relatively simple method of increasing airflow: just increase boost. So, as a tuning method for very high power levels, it is the most cost-effective. Having said that, every engine has limits, and just turning up the boost will at some point destroy the engine, so realistic boundaries have to be set.

If you buy a complete conversion kit, make sure it suits your car. The big difference is between left- and right-hand drive.

For a turbo conversion you will need a turbo, an oil feed from the engine main oil gallery, a free flowing oil drain from the turbo to the sump (above the max oil level line), an intercooler mounted in front of the radiator and any oil coolers or air con radiators, lots of tubing, and either a modified ECU, or, better still, a mappable ECU such as an Emerald.

You then need to make the turbo fit the manifold, or make a new tubular manifold. Bear in mind that the exhaust will be hotter than standard, and there will be a lot of radiating surface area that could be above 800ºC in the engine bay, so heat shielding for pretty much everything that side of the bay is a good idea.

A more or less standard 2.5, running 1 bar boost with something the size of a Garret T3 turbo, and mapped properly, could be expected to make about 350bhp and 360lb-ft at the flywheel.

Problems
Head cracking
High-power M20 engines can crack the cylinder head at the water jacket. There is a weak spot, and some tuners offer a conversion where this area is welded, giving extra strength.

A word of warning: if you have a pre-face-lift M20 engine, take the oil filler cap off and look inside at the cylinder head bolts. Early engines had

bearings and seals fitted, otherwise you are stressing an unknown entity, and any weaknesses in the head gasket, or small cracks in the head or leaking seals, could pressurise the crankcase, blow out the oil, and ruin your day.

A properly rebuilt, boosted M20 engine can run about 400bhp when conventional hex-headed bolts that can fail without warning – the head shears off and can potentially write-off an engine, or at the very least allow coolant to flow up the bolt hole into the oil. Later engines had Torx-headed bolts that stretch slightly when done up ('torque to yield' is the technical term), and can only be used once, so if you need to remove the head again you will need another set of bolts. They can be directly fitted to older engines. Some people have done this without changing the head gasket by replacing one bolt at a time, so that the head remains clamped. This means the whole operation can take less than an hour. Personally, I would rather take off and inspect the head anyway, and fit a new gasket. Either way, the general advice is: if you have the earlier bolts, swap them for the new ones straight away – don't wait for them to fail.

The stretch bolts do need to be set properly using both a torque wrench and an angle gauge.

Another option, particularly if you are planning a lot of work on the engine, is to fit head studs with nuts at the top end. These seem to tolerate more frequent head removal, and are favoured by some race preparation companies.

Another approach that some users have tried is using stock grade 12.9 bolts, 150mm long and partially (lower

Increasing power puts more strain on the engine, including head bolts. The original items are a known weak point, and BMW replaced these hex head bolts with stronger Torx head ones.

The standard cam sprocket has teeth separated by 15 degrees, so, for fine tuning cam timing, an adjustable sprocket is required.

section only) threaded to M10 1.5 pitch, torqued to 80ft-lb. Although I have no independent proof of the long-term usefulness of these, the BMW stretch bolts should, in theory, give a more consistent clamping force.

ENGINE SWAPS
Tuning an engine without spending money is always a challenge. Luckily BMW tends to tune its engines for performance as standard, but there are still a few juicy options for those seeking even higher performance.

Secondhand E30 engines are becoming a little more difficult to come by, so many tuners turn to alternative motors. Modified E30s have been fitted with an amazing range of blocks including later straight-six engines, the M62 V8, and even the outstanding BMW V12. But we should not forget there are many other alternatives, too. How about a Corvette V8, or even a modern high-torque diesel engine?

General guidance
When using an alien engine, it is usually best to get a complete donor car. This means you can check the engine works properly before you go to all the trouble of fitting it. Also, in the UK you need proof of purchase to identify to the authorities where the engine came from, so having all the donor car details is very useful.

Another good reason for getting a complete car is that there are usually a large number of small parts, modules, and connections that will be needed, and just buying an engine on its own often results in many hours tracking down ancillary parts to make it work. I usually use the donor exhaust downpipe

This is the space you have to play with. The biggest problems when fitting large engines come from the heater pipes and the brake servo.

too, and make a custom exhaust using the donor exhaust boxes and new steel tube, although you could purchase a big bore E30 exhaust and make an adaptor. Personally, I keep the donor car until the project car is fully working and on the road, then I know I definitely don't need any more donor parts and the car can be safely disposed of. Unfortunately, this takes a huge amount of space. If that's not available, it is vital to look through all the wiring diagrams, fuel system diagrams, cooling system parts list, etc, to draw up a full list of all the parts you need.

The gearbox

There are two approaches to engine swaps: one is to use the existing gearbox, and the other is to take the donor gearbox. Using the existing gearbox has the advantage that you don't need to modify the gearbox linkages, mounts, and prop shaft, but it does mean that unless you choose an engine that happens to bolt directly to the gearbox, you will need custom adaptor plates (with the centre accurate to within 0.1mm), and a suitable clutch or flex plate. When upgrading to a much more powerful engine, the existing gearbox may not be able to cope anyway, so using the donor car gearbox often makes a better solution.

The radiator

The radiator needs to be sized appropriately for engine power, but this is not as straightforward as you might think. Obviously, actual radiator size is crucial, but the airflow through it is even more important.

The simplest method is to use the cooling system from the donor car, but for race cars I find that a smaller radiator can work just as well, because there is always high airflow (high speed) through the radiator on a track. It only needs a modest electric fan when coming into the pits. My 316 retained its small radiator with integral expansion tank when I fitted the 325 engine for this reason.

This standard 325i shows how little spare room there is between the engine and radiator. Fitting a custom radiator further forward creates a lot more space.

If, however, the car is for road use where it could be stuck in traffic on a hot day, the full donor car cooling system is advisable. With very large engines, such as the BMW V12, there may be very little room left in the engine bay. It is important to ensure the cooling air going into the radiator has somewhere to go, because if it gets blocked by a full engine bay, flow will reduce and the car could overheat. Remember – air has to get into the radiator, but also has to get out.

Fitting a non-standard engine

Although other ways of doing it exist and may be better, the procedure I use is as follows:

1. Take the old engine out of the project car, clean up the engine bay, and check everything that will remain on the car in that area is in good condition. If not, get new parts, but don't fit them just yet.

2. For track and race cars, I spray the engine bay gloss white, as a bright engine bay makes maintenance so much easier later on.

3. Take out and check the donor engine and/or gearbox. Tighten any loose bits and fix any problems.

4. Slowly put the donor engine in the right place in the E30, being careful not to snag any wiring or pipes on the way. At this stage it will become clear whether the bulkhead or trans tunnel needs modifying – if they do, mark out and make sketches of how far things need to be moved. I also sketch out new gearbox mounts and engine mounts, if needed.

5. Whilst the engine is roughly in the right place, check the radiator and other ancillaries fit, and where changes need to be made, make measurements and sketch a diagram.

6. Remove the engine again, fix anything in the engine bay that needs fixing, modify the bulkhead/tunnel if needed, make any brackets needed for the radiator and ancillaries, then make sure the cooling pack parts all fit. Remove the radiator again for safety when installing the engine.

7. Finally, the engine goes in for real. Ensure the engine and gearbox mounts all line up using the new parts as needed.

Engine electrical connections

The E30 has a fuse box in the engine bay and a circular twist lock connector to the engine wiring loom. There are some pin location changes between models, but basically any E30 engine can be connected, as can some other BMW engines, although some variants will need slight wiring modifications.

If using a non-BMW engine, I would cut the engine loom from the E30 original engine, so you have the round connector and half a meter of wire on the engine side to connect into the new engine electrics. (See the electrical section for a connector diagram.)

Another angle shows how the standard sump curves over the steering rack, so whatever you fit, the sump bowl will need to be at the front or, of course, the engine can be dry sumped.

Duel mass flywheels

These are big, heavy and expensive. Early items have a reputation for failure, and many people replace them with conventional solid items, but this is not always a good idea.

A duel mass flywheel (DMF) has the main inertia weight attached via a rubber mounting, so it can absorb the most severe vibrations from the crank. This improves refinement, but does a lot more on modern engine designs where the reduced peak force on the crank allows designers to reduce the main bearing size and make the crank lighter. This results in less engine drag and also reduced inertia, which improves economy by a small fraction, plus it

makes the engine a bit sportier and allows faster gear changes, although the improvement is often quite small. From our point of view, the problem is that some modern engines with cranks designed specifically for a DMF can fail when a solid flywheel is attached. The increased peak forces can crack a DMF crank.

Early engines that were originally designed for a solid flywheel are usually fine, so an M50 engine is often converted from DMF to solid with no issues, but later designs of engine should be fully researched before conversion.

Immobilisers and ECU security

All modern cars have ECU-based security systems that interact with the car's security system and key. A pair of rolling codes which change on each use is sent between the ECU and security system before the engine can start.

Taking an engine from a car with an immobiliser is a problem. One solution is to take the whole system, including all the wiring and security module, and, crucially, the ignition barrel transmitter with the key (transponder) taped to it.

An alternative is to bin the stock ECU and fit an aftermarket programmable ECU such as Emerald or Mega Squirt, and get the engine properly mapped.

The final option is to get the stock ECU set in 'factory mode,' where it will run without a security system, but most

The passenger side engine bracket has plenty of space here ...

ECUs blow an internal link when they first get security enabled and cannot be reset into this mode.

Not all E30 shells are equal ...

There were a few changes to the floorpan layout on the E30 during its production run, which may influence your choice of replacement engine.

The key differences are between the face-lift cars and older ones, and between the small 4-cylinder cars and the rest. The main differences to look for are the prop shaft centre bearing mounting point (a face-lift car's mounting point is higher off the ground, and bolt holes further outboard from the centre), the radiator mounting bracket (radiators are different shapes, 4-cylinder face-lift car has shallower and wider radiator), and radiator expansion tank (4-cylinder face-lift has integral expansion tank on the radiator, so has no mounting point for the wing-mounted expansion tank).

Fitting an M30 engine

The old BMW 'big six' engine was fitted as standard by BMW South Africa in the 333, and makes for a very fast car, although the extra 25kg of weight (compared to an M20) will affect handling to some extent.

M30 engines were available in the 6 Series ('78-'82). A slightly lower power version (although most people wouldn't notice the small difference) was in the E23, E24 and E28 ('82-'87), but a third generation M30 is possibly the most

... unlike the driver's side, which has to negotiate the steering column.

One popular donor is the 635 or 535i with the big six M30 engine. When using a donor, it is worth harvesting all of the ancillary parts as well as the engine. I always keep the donor car until the project car is properly up and running.

Jim Cameron's 335 shows a very neat M30 installation, very similar to that of qthe Alpina. (Courtesy Jim Cameron)

desirable, with 1mm larger intake valves, increased compression ratio, and a few other improvements. This appeared in the E32 and E34 ('87-'92). Also, the

E32/43 engine has a sump that fits in the E30, but the older engines will foul the steering rack unless the engine is mounted significantly rearwards.

If using the donor gearbox, you will need to shorten the gear linkage and prop shaft

Alpina made a few E30 big sixes, the B6, with the engine mounted far forward. This means there are Alpina engine mounts etc available, but they are very rare. Early Alpinas had the engine as far forward as possible, which required a special radiator mounted further forward, and an electric fan mounted to the front of the new radiator. It was a curious choice of position – you can't really get any further forward, and whilst it does allow for easy clutch changes, the handling is very nose-heavy. Their later (post '87) cars had the engine slightly further back. This position still does not need bulkhead modifications, and can be recreated using an E28 535i radiator, which is a bolt-in fit for most 6-cylinder E30 shells, but the distributor cap ends up about a centimetre away from the

radiator, so a front-mounted electric fan is still required, and the water pump connection needs to be modified.

If you are not afraid of modifying the bodywork, a better solution is to recess the bulkhead around the cylinder head area by about 6cm, allowing enough room for engine rock. This gives a weight distribution similar to the 325 (assuming boot-mounted battery), and allows the fitting of the full 535 cooling pack with engine-driven fan, if desired.

The custom 335 exhaust manifold flows beautifully past the Alpina-style engine mounts and the steering components. (Courtesy Jim Cameron)

M50/52

Of course, the M30 is pretty old now, and many modifiers go for the later M50 or M52 six, using an engine from an E34 5 Series puts the sump pan at the right end, oddly the E36 3 Series engines wont fit because their sump pans are at the wrong end, however an E36 M3 exhaust manifold locates the downpipe in the right place. For left-hand drive cars the brake booster interferes with the engine. It is possible to relocate it and use a longer operating shaft, but as ever don't take any risks with the brakes. Many people use the E34

This superb V8 installation uses the donor car cooling pack and header tank. Note the custom remote oil filter and PAS reservoir bracket and the throttle cable; also that there is no space for the brake servo.

throttle cable to go between the M50 throttle and the E30 pedal.

The E34 M50 engine mounts apparently fit the E30 subframe. Alternatives include E28 533i mounts with 5mm spacers, or E28 M5 mounts. The M50 can also take the solid flywheel from an M20 engine, giving a few more options for a suitable gearbox.

This is the engine era in which immobilisers were introduced. For, simplicity, avoid silver label '413' motronic with EWS (security).

BMW V8, M60/62

There are a lot of options here: with or without the VANOS variable cam timing system, capacities of 3.0, 3.5, 4.0 and 4.4, plus a huge range of auto and manual gearboxes (including 6-speed options).

The V8 is a slightly taller engine,

and the sump wants to hit the front subframe. Many modifiers drop the subframe by using ally spacers on the chassis rails, and then using lower springs. V8s from E32, E34, and E38 need no changes to the sump. Other models have the pan too far back.

As with the M30 engine, the E28 535i radiator is a popular choice, and fits directly in some E30 shells. With the V8 mounted as close as possible to the bulkhead, there will only be a few centimetres clearance to the radiator, so the engine driven fan does not fit.

The exhaust is very tight. Some people report good results using E39 or X5 manifolds, others prefer custom headers, but whichever route you go there will be welding involved.

On RHD cars the brake servo is very close to the rocker cover, but on LHD cars there is no room at all for it. A

replacement servo unit is often remotely mounted at the front of the left-hand inner wing.

The brake servo problem has been resolved with this race-style pedal box with adjustable brake bias. Note the neat strut tower reinforcement plates.

BMW V12

Should be easy – after all, it's just another row of six cylinders! Well, almost. Unfortunately it is longer than an M30, as the banks are staggered. The V12 can be fitted with a more or less standard bulkhead, but with no room for the standard radiator, which has to be moved further forwards with an electric fan mounted in front. There is no room for the standard brake servo – a racing pedal box can solve the problem if you fancy non-assisted brakes, otherwise a remote-mounted servo just behind the headlight is probably the only other option. There is just enough space to get two airboxes in, but not if you have a remote brake servo.

The plus side is that the V12 only weighs about 7kg more than an M30, depending on which flavour engine you use, so it can make a surprisingly nimble fast car.

Other engine manufacturers

Some people have used the Corvette

It's the details that make the difference, like getting the right engine mounts. These two are both E30. The later 4-cylinder item has a large void for refinement, but has less bonding area between metal and rubber, which means they it is weaker.

LS1 V8 in alloy form, which weighs about 170kg and is available in powers from 300bhp to about 405bhp: a pretty good power/weight trade off. They are reasonably priced and have huge tuning potential. There is a range of gearboxes available, including the Borg Warner T6 manual 6-speed. Obviously nothing fits immediately, but these sorts of engines are fairly compact and shorter than a straight six.

There is a similar argument for the Ford Mustang engine, and many other high-power US V8s.

The British Jaguar V8 is also well worth considering, especially in supercharged form (225kg and 420bhp). Replacing the supercharger with a pair of turbos releases another 80bhp and saves weight, making +500bhp quite achievable.

There is also an immense range of very high-power Japanese engines. 4-cylinder turbo units offer high power and low weight, and some of the 6-cylinder engines have been tuned to well above 1000bhp.

In fact the options available are mind boggling, as long as you have the resources to make the mounts, cooling system, electrics etc.

BMW engine weights and powers (approximate)

4-cylinder engines		
M10	83kg	1.5 (75bhp), 1.6 (85bhp), 1.8 (90-98bhp), 2.0 (100bhp), 2.0i (125bhp), 2.0Tii (130bhp), 2.0 turbo (170bhp)
M40	81kg	1.6 (102bhp), 1.8 (122bhp)
M42	100kg	1.8 (138-142bhp)
M43	83kg	1.6 (102bhp), 1.8 (115bhp), 1.9 (118bhp)
M44	102kg	1.9 (142-150bhp)

6-cylinder engines		
M20	117kg	2.0i (129bhp), 2.3i (143bhp), 2.5i (170bhp), 2.7e (125bhp)
M30	143kg	2.5i (150bhp), 2.8i (184bhp), 3.0 (185-208bhp), 3.3 (200-206bhp), 3.5 (218bhp)
M102	145kg	3.2 or 3.4 Turbo (252bhp)
M50	136kg	2.0 (150bhp), 2.5 (192bhp), 3.0 (240bhp)
M52	118kg (alloy block) / 140kg (US iron block)	2.0 (150bhp), 2.5 (170bhp), 2.8 (193bhp), 3.2 (240bhp)
M54	126kg	2.0 (150bhp), 2.2 (170bhp), 2.5 (184-192bhp), 2.8 (193bhp), 3.0 (231bhp)
M56	127kg	2.5 (184bhp)

8-cylinder engines		
M60	146kg	3.0 (218bhp), 4.0 (286bhp)
M62	140kg	3.5 (235bhp), 4.4 (286bhp), 4.6 (340bhp)

12-cylinder engines		
M70	155kg	5.0 (300bhp)
M73	150kg	5.4 (326bhp)

TURBO AND SUPERCHARGING

Undoubtedly this is the most effective way of getting more air into an engine, and with secondhand turbo and

These days there is a huge selection of turbos available, with an equally huge range of characteristics. Make sure you get the right sort for your application.

Simple waste-gated turbos can use a boost capsule like this. The rod has an adjusting screw, and lengthening it will increase boost pressure.

This is a Roots-type supercharger made by Eaton. Again, these are readily available secondhand, but you need the right sort for your application.

superchargers being so common, it can be a very economical way of getting significantly more power. But force-feeding an engine that was never designed for it does bring many challenges – get it wrong, and the engine can be destroyed in seconds.

Basic principle

When tuning a naturally aspirated engine, the art is to use a cam that creates a depression in the exhaust just as the exhaust valve opens, and a pressure wave just in front of the intake as it opens. As it is easier to force out pressurised exhaust gas than draw in low pressure air, the exhaust valve is smaller than the intake valve. However, boosted engines change this equation. The cam no longer has to generate the flow, because the turbo or supercharger is creating all the pressure needed when on boost. The large overlap that a naturally aspirated race engine cam has is also no longer needed – in fact, it can be a hindrance, because the compressor can just blow straight through the engine into the exhaust wasting mixture, so less overlap is needed.

What you end up with is more like a standard production cam, or even one that would normally produce more low-end torque at the expense of top-end power – that way the engine is naturally torquey low down, which helps with turbos or superchargers that have little low rpm boost.

To hold things together, there are a few things to sort out:

Cooling. The system is designed to take away a given amount of heat energy. If you double the power, you double the heat to be removed. The cylinder head, particularly round the high-temperature exhaust valve seat, can transmit a set amount of energy into the coolant in a set time. When overwhelmed, the coolant starts to boil around the hot spots. You won't know about this immediately because the rest of the coolant may be fine, but this localised boiling allows the exhaust valve to overheat and burn out, so the first thing you know about it is when the engine starts knocking or drops a valve.

The first step on very high-power engines is to ensure there is nothing coating the cooling passages. Tap

water has minerals in that coat the inner passages just like a kettle element, and they need to be removed in the same way.

For very high-powered engines the exhaust valves can be replaced with sodium-filled items. These have a hollow shaft with a sodium compound that transfers heat from the valve head to the shaft, and then through the valve guide. The only drawback is that they are quite expensive.

The pistons get hot, too. One way to remove heat directly from the piston crown is to use oil spray jets. These are a standard fitment on many modern engines, but on an old E30 engine considerable engineering has to be done to get them in – usually tapping off the oil gallery where it feeds the main bearings. An alternative is to use con rods that have a special drilling, which allows oil from the big end bearing to flow up the rod, around a groove at the gudgeon pin, and out of a small hole in the top. Either way, the oil gets hotter, so improved oil cooling is also essential for high-powered engines.

Turbo lag

As the boost level depends on the exhaust flow, when you suddenly floor the throttle there is a short pause as the turbine spins up. This is turbo lag, and is worse with very big turbos. Contrary to popular belief, the length of the intake tubing makes only a very small difference to lag – usually so small it's not noticeable. Each bhp uses about a pint of fresh air every second, so for 300bhp there will be about 300 pints a second flowing in, and a change in intake system volume of a pint or two will make very little difference. That means you can mount the turbo where it fits best, and run as much tubing as needed to get to the intercooler and back.

Small turbos spin up faster and reduce lag. It's best to get a turbo that is just big enough for your target power level, otherwise you'll get too much lag, then have to dump excess boost pressure.

Gas

Turbos and nitrous oxide work very well. The Nos jets cool the air, a bit like having a better intercooler, and the instant power increase combats turbo lag.

Intercooler

As the intake air is compressed, it gets hotter, but hot air is less dense, which reduces power, so it has to be cooled again in an intercooler, aka a chargecooler. The amount of cooling depends on the mass flow rate of the air and the boost pressure, and it's the same story for turbos and superchargers.

For very light boost levels, the heating effect may be acceptable, and the complexity of an intercooler may be avoided – as a rough guide, less than 0.5 bar usually doesn't require an intercooler. The intercooler has to be cooled down by either fresh air from the front of the car rushing through its fins (air-to-air intercooler), or by water pumped around its own circuit by a separate intercooler pump, with small water radiators usually mounted just behind the front bumper (air-to-water intercooler). Air-to-air coolers are lighter, simpler, and cheaper, but air-to-water intercoolers can be more effective, especially at very high boost levels, and also allow the cooler to be located in the intake manifold.

Bearings and oil feed

Holding a turbo together at up to 220,000rpm needs very good bearings.

Most turbos rely on a thin film of high-pressure oil in a plain bearing. These generally need a minimum of about 20psi oil pressure within a few seconds of starting, and about 30psi minimum at full load. Some can cope with a minimum of about 10psi at idle, but check for the exact turbo you intend to use. Plain bearing turbos need an oil feed rate of about 2 to 4 litres a minute, depending on load, so usually their oil feed is tapped into the main oil gallery, but a separate electric oil pump is a possible solution for remote-mounted turbos.

There are all sorts of shapes and sizes of intercooler available – the lower one here is from a Mondeo diesel; the upper one from a Volvo 940.

Some turbos have ball bearings, which last longer and spin up much faster. Their oil feeds have a small restriction to keep the pressure down to prevent oil leaks. The oil flow just needs to be enough to prevent the bearing cooking. Oil feed requirements for a ball bearing turbo are very different to a plain bearing one.

Both types need a good flow of oil to keep cool, otherwise the oil cooks. That's why it's a good idea to let a turbo engine idle for a moment before switching off, to let the turbo slow down. Some people even fit separate electrical oil pumps that feed the turbo for a few seconds after the engine has stopped.

High-performance turbos also have water cooling in the bearing housing, which helps prevent the oil burning up.

The oil drain must flow freely and have no restriction, so if plumbing it back to the sump it really needs to be at least 50mm above the highest oil level. If it ends up submerged, the flow can back up and the bearing start to cook.

Heat

The exhaust manifold can glow bright white on performance cars at full tilt – that's over 1100°C – so the turbo gets hot, the engine gets hot, everything gets hot. For best performance, therefore, the air intake needs to come from the front of the car, away from the heat of the engine bay. There also needs to be adequate heat shields to prevent other components in the engine bay cooking. The heat radiates into the fuel, which can lead to vapour locks and trouble starting a hot engine. It also heats the electrics and belts, making everything wear out faster. It may be worth fitting vents in the bonnet above the turbo, and wrapping the exhaust in thermal cloth can help, too.

Compression

Compressing air makes it hot. If the air/fuel mixture in the cylinder is compressed too much, it gets hot enough to explode. Detonation can melt pistons, which is bad, so turbo engines have lower compression ratios than naturally aspirated engines. However, go too low and you lose efficiency and power. 8.5:1 is the lowest for most applications.

Turbo size

Turbos are usually referred to by their frame size and the aspect ratio (A/R) of each wheel. Basically, a bigger frame size is a bigger turbo, and a bigger A/R gives more power but worse lag.

If the turbo is too big, it never gets up to speed. If the turbo is too small, it can't keep up, may overspeed, hits the damaging surge zone, and the pressure stays low.

Tail mount turbo

A new trend is to fit turbos on naturally aspirated engines right at the back of the exhaust system, running low boost levels up to about 0.5 bar. It's just enough boost to make a useful performance improvement without needing any big engine modifications or an intercooler.

Intake hoses

Standard road cars have rubber hoses in the intake system, good for temperatures up to about 120°C. On some race cars the engine bay temperature can get higher, so silicone hoses are needed. The problem with silicone is that it is very slippery and can pop off the turbo or tubework with no warning, so the metal tubes need to have a good size securing bead and a good quality hose clamp to hold the silicone hose on. By the way, some inferior hose clamps can pinch the hose near the worm drive, leaving a small leak, so don't buy cheap ones.

Turbo or supercharged E30s work very well. Both M10 and M20 engines take to turbocharging very well, even with standard spec engines as long as they are well built. The head weakness of M40 engines makes them a little less appealing for boosting, but low pressure systems can make a useful increase across the rev range. The M42 is a better choice, as long as the cooling system is engineered to cope.

There is usually sufficient space

in an E30 to bolt a supercharger to the side of the engine, but they do need a substantial drivebelt system. Eaton M Series superchargers are usually geared to run between 2 and 3 times faster than the engine, and the drivebelt has to transmit a fair amount of power. An M112 at full load may need over 80bhp from the drivebelt!

The abundance of superchargers, such as the Eaton M45 from BMW Minis, makes them an affordable addition to the E30 4-cylinder engines, providing the potential to outperform a standard 325i. However, the charger drive and intercooler makes the weight similiar to that of a standard M20 engine.

Supercharging the M20 can yield substantially higher power – up to 400bhp may be possible, and of course, if you have put in an even bigger engine there is even more potential. Here are some rough power figures for the Eaton M Series (the number after the M refers to approximate cubic inches of air per rev of the 'charger'):

M45	220bhp
M62	300bhp
M90	430bhp
M112	540bhp

By comparison, turbochargers are about 15kg lighter than an equivalent supercharger, so for M10 and M42 engines a turbo makes more sense.

Turbos have been around for many years, and there are some good secondhand bargains to be had. Again, the size of the turbo relates to maximum airflow. Taking the old Garret T Series of turbos as an example, where the number after the 'T' referred to approximate wheel diameter in inches or tenths of inches, here are some very approximate maximum power figures:

T17	200bhp
T25	250bhp
T3	340bhp
T4	500bhp

Finding somewhere to put the intercooler can be tricky. As it needs plenty of cool air, there is a trend for external mounting, but this method brings a big risk of damage from road debris and/or clogging with dirt.

The BMW in-line engines, with exhaust and intake on opposite sides, lend themselves to turbos. This turbo M30 in an E21 uses a high-mounted turbo and up-swept exhaust manifold, avoiding a clash with the steering column.

Efficiency and power consumed by the turbocharger

In all cases, compressing air requires power, which can only come from the engine burning fuel. A turbo does use some of the energy normally wasted in the exhaust, but still puts a greater demand on the engine, too. The back pressure goes up, and the engine works harder to push out the gas. By comparison, the supercharger uses none of the usually wasted power, and all of its power comes from the engine burning fuel. For instance a high-power M20 engine running an Eaton M112 supercharger could be producing, say, 420bhp at the flywheel, but 80bhp will also be used in the supercharger drive at the front, so the pistons are actually producing the equivalent of 500bhp. However, swapping from a supercharger to a Garret T40 turbo will not liberate all of that 80bhp – depending on valve/cam etc it may only liberate 40bhp. In the turbo engine, the pistons may still be producing about 500bhp, but roughly 40bhp will be used on the exhaust stroke overcoming back pressure, so at the flywheel you may see 460bhp.

Cheap alternatives and small electric 'superchargers'

As you can see from the previous paragraphs, the work a supercharger or turbo does compressing large volumes of air takes a lot of power – that's just the laws of nature. In both cases, some of the power driving the compressor is wasted as heat – a supercharger may have a peak efficiency of only 67%, and a turbo about 75%. Some people have tried using electric motors to drive the compressors, as they can be up to 90% efficient. However, it's not that simple.

Even boosting a 4-cylinder E30 engine to about 200bhp will require at least 30bhp of power to compress the air. 30bhp is 40kw, so if the electrical system is running at 14v, that would need an electrical motor driving the fan, which takes nearly three thousand amps! By comparison, an E30 starter motor, which is quite a big, requires about 2kw.

So when you see adverts for miraculously cheap superchargers – particularly small electric fans that look suspiciously similar to computer fans – you need to be realistic.

ALTERNATIVE FUELS
Petrol/diesel prices will only ever go up, so there's increasing pressure to find alternatives on which to run classic cars.

Petrol engines
LPG (Liquefied Petroleum Gas) is a mix of butane and propane that turns to liquid when compressed to about 5 bar, depending on temperature. When released to atmospheric pressure, it reverts to a gaseous state and mixes very well with air to form a combustible mixture. Petrol is a natural liquid, and no matter how fine the injected spray, there will always be some droplets that won't completely combust, leading to carbon deposits and hydrocarbon (HC) emissions. LPG, however, is already a gas when taken into the engine, so the HC emissions can be reduced. This also results in much lower carbon deposits and almost no oil contamination. It has a higher knock resistance (octane rating), suiting turbo and high compression engines. But the overriding reason most people convert to LPG is that it is half the cost of petrol, mostly due to lower taxation.

In an E30, the economics of

These Kehin LPG injectors are used by some car manufacturers, and offer high quality and reliability. They can be controlled by an aftermarket ECU such as the Megasquirt unit, making a custom installation quite tempting.

converting to LPG do not usually stack up. A decent kit will cost over £1000, so the car would have to drive a great many miles before the savings paid for the conversion.

From a performance point of view, the story is a little different. The higher octane rating, if combined with higher compression ratio (potentially over 11:1), can make a fairly high-power engine, and it also suits turbo engines running higher boost levels.

LPG's burn rate is slower, so the ignition must be advanced to get the best out of it, otherwise it is effectively running retarded and the exhaust valves could suffer. It also does not provide the cushioning of the valve seats that petrol does, so harder valve seats may be a good idea if the engine does a lot of miles flat out, such as in a race or track car. Another solution is to use a valve lube dispensing system, which dribbles a tiny amount of fluid into the intake as the engine is running – however, every example I have seen distributes the fluid unevenly, leaving some cylinders dryer than others, and I would question their effectiveness.

Buying a pre-converted car can be much cheaper, but there are still potential problems. Over the years I have trained many LPG fitters and examined many converted cars, and one thing that strikes me is just how many cars are badly converted, often with bad electrical connections and an incorrect mixture, leading to backfires and high fuel consumption. A properly converted car will use more LPG than petrol, but no more than 10 to 20%. Any higher indicates the system is set too rich, probably to cover up other problems. An engine that has been converted mechanically for LPG with higher compression and advanced ignition should match or even improve on the petrol MPG figure.

Done well, LPG is a very good fuel. I have converted a small fleet of race cars for use as hired-out trackday cars for a well-known British race circuit. They averaged 25 thousand

miles a year flat out, and compared to their petrol equivalents, the engine wear was reduced, failures were less frequent, and the oil change requirement were drastically reduced. But these conversions cost over £10,000 each!

If you are doing a conversion yourself, make sure you are properly trained. Advice is available from the LPG Association in the UK, which operates a strict code of practice (CoP) that is vital to ensure safety and quality. Other countries have similar organisations.

If you know what you are doing, LPG can be a great performance fuel; if you don't, it can be a nightmare, and is best left to the experts.

Ethanol/bioethanol

Fuel made from plants is gaining interest worldwide, although there are commercial and political issues still to be resolved. Ideally we would use 'phase 2' ethanol, which is made by 'cracking' waste food and the stuff left over from regular food production, but this is an expensive process at the moment. Most ethanol is brewed from maze or other types of food, which technically takes food away from us and raises food prices. Because of these factors, the price of ethanol may vary dramatically over time, but at some point in the future will probably become reasonably cheap.

More importantly, as a fuel it has some advantages, already comprising between 5 and 10% of the content of ordinary pump petrol in the UK. In Brazil, ethanol forms 25% of petrol. All modern cars are tested to work perfectly with 10% ethanol. So, to an extent, you are already running on ethanol.

Ethanol has about 34% less energy per litre than petrol, so you need to burn more of it to do the same work, and MPG will be worse on a standard engine. If you are converting to neat ethanol, you will need to increase fuelling by about 51% to compensate, but it has a very high octane rating, and so, just like with LPG,

an engine converted to run a suitably high compression ratio will take full advantage of the fuel, and can actually make better MPG than a standard petrol engine. As a race fuel it offers higher power outputs than petrol, and is used in many race series.

There are two problems with ethanol on E30s. First, it is hygroscopic, and the absorbed water can cause problems. It can attack some types of metal, most notably steel, on which any sort of corrosion results in strong acids forming. Second, ethanol eats into some types of rubber, so the E30 fuel tank, fuel lines, fuel rail, etc, should be replaced with stainless or ethanol-resistant tubing. It can also eat through exhaust systems, so a full stainless steel exhaust, including manifolds, may be a good idea. The Bosch in-line fuel pump has been used successfully with ethanol, although the fact ethanol is conductive means the motor has a hard time and durability suffers.

Neat ethanol can also eat into aluminium, and has been cited as the cause of damage to cylinder heads. However if there is about 1% water, which is often the case anyway, then this problem is solved (see SAE paper 2005-01-3708).

An important practical problem is that ethanol really doesn't mix well with air. When cold it gets much worse, and below -12°C you need engine heaters to stand any chance of starting the car. That is why 100% ethanol, known as E100, is rarely used. Most forecourt blends have some petrol in to assist starting, and the most common is E85, which is 85% ethanol and 15% petrol. However, ethanol is soluble in water, and petrol less so. The result is that, given enough time (a period of months), it will absorb enough moisture from the air to separate into a layer of petrol and a layer of watery ethanol. This means it is a matter of pure chance as to which fuel goes down the fuel line to the engine, and your new engine tune is rendered useless, potentially causing detonation. The shelf life of E85 is about 90 days.

As well as the revised fuel tank and fuel lines, to convert an E30 you will need bigger, ethanol-tolerant injectors, fuel rail, pressure regulator, and new ignition and fuel maps.

Methanol is available in some countries. It has many of the same problems as ethanol, but also has a lower power potential, so it is not usually considered a performance fuel. It is not to be confused with nitromethane, which is a race fuel used by Top Fuel drag racers. This is a highly noxious fuel that contains oxygen. It has immense power potential, but costs a fortune and is very difficult to work with. It is unlikely to be a practical option for an E30 unless running a many-thousand-bhp drag engine!

Diesel engines

LPG can be added to an M21 diesel with good results. A very small amount is added to the intake, which increases burn speed of the diesel fuel. This increases the energy released by the diesel that is turned into useful power. The standard M21 turbo engine power could potentially be raised to around 160bhp, with a large spread of usable power over the whole rev range, plus much reduced turbo lag. Potentially, performance could be similar to a 325i.

In addition the combined fuel economy, including the cost of the LPG used, can also improve by over 10%, potentially giving 50mpg.

The downside is that the system has to be mapped properly. Getting the calibration wrong and putting in a touch too much LPG will melt pistons!

Bio-diesel and reclaimed cooking oil

The simplicity of the M21 engines means that they are reasonably tolerant of poor quality fuel, so running on reclaimed cooking oil is possible. However, these 'dirty' fuels still result in higher carbon deposits in the engine, the trapped water can rot the

fuel system, and cold starting can be difficult.

Genuine bio-diesel is effectively the same as regular diesel, the main problem being microscopic organisms tend to like growing in it, and then clogging the fuel filter and pump. A tank of bio-diesel should not be kept for more than about six months, which can be a problem on a classic car that doesn't get used much.

EXHAUST

BMW has always tuned its road cars for performance and the standard exhaust manifold and system are very good. Changes made in 1988 to the M20 made the manifold even better. Altering any part of the exhaust without other engine modifications is unlikely to make any real performance gain, although removing one of the mufflers and fitting a straight-through pipe will make the car slightly lighter and sound a little more sporty. So, a general rule of thumb: if you are only increasing power by 10%, there is little to be gained from modifying the exhaust on an E30.

Having said that, an old muffler can collapse inside, which could potentially block the flow. Obviously in this case replacing it with a new standard box would restore performance to the original level, but genuine parts are quite expensive, so if you have to replace a muffler anyway then it may be worth considering a sportier alternative.

Not all louder mufflers have better flow. I have seen some designs that are both loud and restrictive. There is a lot of science in good muffler design, and unfortunately, some of the less renowned exhaust companies appear to lack the correct knowledge.

Basically there are two types of muffler: the absorption type uses perforated tube wrapped in fibre matting to absorb higher frequencies, whereas the labyrinth type uses a sort of maze to cause lower frequency sound waves to be disrupted. Both convert sound energy into heat. A car exhaust system is designed with both types to

The more power you have, the more heat comes out of the tail pipe. This car has a metal plate to protect the rear valance. (Courtesy Jim Cameron)

Don't lose sight of the fact that a track or race car still has to comply with noise limits. Keeping it quiet need not reduce power, if done correctly.

cover the key noise frequencies. Their distance from the engine is important, as it determines standing wave frequencies, so really both mufflers and the connecting pipes work together as a system. The bodyshell is a box too, just like a guitar body, and it has a resonant frequency of its own, which the standard exhaust system is specifically designed to avoid 'setting off.'

Designing a sports exhaust system can be tricky. If any of the design factors are compromised, some frequencies can become dominant, and the exhaust can boom or howl at certain engine speeds, making motorway driving quite unpleasant.

Pulse tuning

From a performance point of view, all

these resonant frequencies are critical to the engine tune.

If you arrange the pipe lengths just right, as soon as the exhaust valve opens a returning negative wave appears and helps to suck the exhaust out – brilliant. But, if the engine speeds up or slows down much, timing goes out the window. The worst case is the positive pressure wave hitting just as the valve opens, blowing the exhaust gas back into the cylinder.

So, for ultimate pulse tuning you end up with a very narrow power band. This means that you need lots of gears in order to stay on the boil, and you could argue that your exhaust design is dictated by your gearbox, amongst many other factors.

You could get rid of the peakiness by reducing the exhaust pulse strength, disrupting the pulses and smoothing things out. This will give a greater spread of power and may well improve real world performance, even though the peak power figure is lower. To do this, arrange the primary exhaust manifold pipes to join in groups of two. Four pipes from a 4-cylinder engine leading

A tubular exhaust manifold not only improves performance, but also looks superb. (Courtesy Jim Cameron)

A common problem with lowered cars – here, the centre box has been frequently scraped on raised surfaces, but it can't be raised because of the prop centre bearing. (Courtesy Jim Cameron)

to two downpipes (four into two), or for the 6-cylinder engine, leading to two groups of three (six into two). The two downpipes combine to form a single exhaust pipe on low-power models, but are kept as two pipes all

the way through on high-power models, although the flows are allowed to mix at the first exhaust muffler.

A sensible exhaust manifold is

A good budget way of making your own exhaust is to buy ready-made bends and weld the system in sections. (Courtesy Jim Cameron)

One solution is to split the box in two, each side of the bearing. (Courtesy Jim Cameron)

big enough to allow good flow, but narrow enough to encourage good gas velocity and ensure it all goes in the same direction. You don't actually want any back pressure as such, but you will find that a good system will inherently generate some due to the narrowness of the bore.

With turbos it all changes. You can get away with poor manifolding to a greater extent due to the sound waves getting mashed in the turbine, so there is very little pulse tuning available. The turbine is sensitive to the pressure difference between the manifold side and downpipe, and it's this difference that generates the force, so you need to ensure the gas can escape easily and the downpipe can make a noticeable difference.

Again, this must work with the rest of the vehicle. Tight turns are not a problem, as gas is quite flexible, but sharp edges and changes in bore will cause turbulence and reduce the flow. Smooth and consistent are good.

Most V8s – such as the M62 – benefit from having a cross-over pipe just after the bell-housing. This is due to the firing sequence being spread across both banks, such that each bank has an uneven sequence, with two neighbouring cylinders firing one after the other followed by a long gap. The cross-over pipe allows some degree of balancing between banks. There is not much total flow in the pipe itself, so it doesn't need to be very big, but where you put it influences the speed at which it has an effect, a bit like a trombone.

There are a few V8s with flat plane cranks that work like two 4-cylinder engines side by side, and these don't need a balance tube. No other type of engine (V12, V6, etc) needs one either.

Heat

Exhaust wrap does not in itself make the car go faster. However, it can help to reduce engine bay temperature, and if your airbox is in cooler air you can get more power – but only a little bit. It is quite fiddly to fit properly, and has

a tendency to fall off. It's also quite expensive, and often a bonnet vent will do a better job. Ceramic coatings are much the same, but more expensive, although prices are dropping.

Exhaust pipe bore

Look at an F1 exhaust. Unless you actually have an F1 engine, you don't need one that big.

Generally the primary pipes should be the same diameter as the exhaust ports, so there is no ledge between port and manifold to generate turbulence. It should start off the same shape as the port to.

The system pipes need to be bigger than the primary's, but not by huge amounts. Remember: each primary is only carrying a wodge of exhaust gas during the exhaust stroke; the rest of the time the gas flow is slowing down and just hanging about. So, the system pipe on a simple four-into-one system could be the same size as the primary's, with only a small loss in total flow. In practice you would make the system pipe about 1.5 to 2 times the primary size for a simple four-into-one, but it depends on the speed of the gas. The faster it started, the more quickly drag slows it down, so the system would benefit more from a bigger bore than if you started with slow velocities. The upshot is, it varies from one sort of engine to another.

As a very rough rule of thumb, a single system pipe diameter would increase as follows:
100bhp = 1.5in
200bhp = 2.75in
300bhp = 3.5in
400bhp = 4.25in
For twin pipe systems, you could work on each pipe being approximately 80% of the above.

Catalysts

Most catalysts are not too bad for power, but if you have reworked the engine for more power (and therefore gas flow), there may be a small gain to be had by removing it.

Downpipes of the correct bore are crucial to performance. (Courtesy Jim Cameron)

Stainless steel

The original E30 exhaust was mild steel treated with an aluminised corrosion protection coating. These generally last about three to five years on British roads. For better long-term reliability of the exhaust, many people swap to a stainless steel system, but beware: there are many grades of stainless steel, and some will corrode faster than a good quality, mild steel system!

A stainless steel system will sound different to a mild steel system, even if all the parts use exactly the same design. This is because stainless is stiffer than mild steel, the frequency that the metal vibrates at is higher, and it transmits more noise through its stiffer walls. For this reason, a good system will use a different design to an equivalent mild steel system. On a sports exhaust systems there will be more 'rasp' and less 'boom.'

Also, as the material is harder it is more difficult to form. Cheaper systems can be awkward to fit, as joints may not line up.

As ever, a quality system is often better value than a cheap one.

Side exit

You may have seen race cars with side exit exhausts, just ahead of the rear wheel under the sill. The advantage is that this system does not have to go through the rear axle assembly, making servicing the axle easier. Also, the shorter system weighs less.

Where race regulations allow, this can be a handy way of simplifying the exhaust system. There's still space on an E30 to fit a good muffler, so although it will be louder than stock, it doesn't have to be excessively noisy. However, there are downsides.

Firstly, there is a potential for fumes to enter the cabin. At racing speeds, the exhaust gas is usually rapidly dispersed, but when coming into the pits or parked and idling, the gas can find its way in through door seals and small gaps. Also, the pipes pass under the sill and make this area quite hot, which can compromise corrosion protection. Ground clearance is also compromised – on a lowered race car, the lower edge can be less than an inch off the ground, and can be damaged if the rear wheel dips into a pothole. For this reason it is not such a great idea for road cars.

This shows a side exit exhaust being mocked up. Simple 'cut and shut' modification is a good way to check your design before committing to the expense of getting a custom system made.

INTAKE TUNING

The standard E30 intake system is actually quite well designed. It takes air

The M3 works racer used larger throttle bodies, airbox, and a cold air induction pipe from the front valance. (Courtesy BMW)

from a shroud round the back of the left headlight, which ensures air entering the engine comes from outside the bay. After a couple of laps on a race circuit the engine, and particularly the exhaust manifold, are stinking hot – engine bay air temperature can easily exceed 100°C, making it much less dense. An intake sourcing air from here would reduce engine power significantly.

Many people modify or remove the standard airbox, which can be a bad thing. For instance, if you remove the internal ram air cone, you will lose about 10lb-ft from a standard 325i. Some people put holes in the airbox base to let more air in, but this will be hot air from inside the engine bay, and again, could reduce power once the engine is hot.

Of course, if the car is for road use only, the under-bonnet temperature may never get high enough to be a problem, so the ideal intake system really does depend on the intended use for the car.

Maximising flow
Maximum flow potential requires

A good intake system should have no steps in the joins, and allow for engine movement. (Courtesy Jim Cameron)

minimum turbulence. The standard ram air cone in the airbox guides the air going into the tube, so the full width inside the tube has maximum flow. If BMW had just used a straight pipe cut off with no flaring at the end, as the air is pulled in over the edge of the pipe it would begin tumbling. This turbulent air would use lots of energy just going round in tight little circles as it tumbles down the inner sides of the pipe, leaving only the centre core of the air flowing properly, therefore potentially flowing only half the air of a properly flared pipe.

Of course, one way round this is to simply use a pipe twice as wide so that turbulence doesn't matter. But that is rarely a practical solution.

Interestingly, the intake can have lots of bends in it without causing too much of a problem. As long as the inside of the ducting is smooth and turbulence free, it can be as complicated as you like; air is very flexible, after all. A smooth, 90° elbow is not restrictive, but a joint with a nasty step in it is, because the step causes turbulence and reduces the effective pipe bore.

A simple cold air intake formed after removing the left-hand main beam headlight. Ducting secured to the headlight support.

The standard M20 intake manifold is well designed, but prone to leaks from the many tubes and hoses that perish and crack.

The ducting feeds into the airbox and is secured to prevent hot engine bay air leaking in.

So, in summary, the secret to an efficient race intake is a smooth path, with cold air from in front of the car.

Cold air intake
A popular method of gaining lots of cold fresh air is to remove the left-hand main beam light unit and fit a large ram pipe in the convenient 4in hole. People fitting V engines may wish to remove both main beam units. But if the vehicle is a road car, check the lighting regulations in your country to make sure it is legal. Obviously, with both main beams removed you'd need to fit auxiliary main beam units to stay safe and be legal on the public roads.

It is interesting to note that BMW Motorsport did not use this method, even on its 370bhp M3 Touring Car racers, but instead ducted in cold air from under the front bumper.

It is also worth noting that the standard shroud around the back of the headlight method worked fine for the road-going M3 with 238bhp, so the stock intake has good potential for modestly-tuned engines.

Air filters
The stock paper air filter element is also surprisingly efficient, but only when new. A sponge or performance cotton filter will maintain high flow for longer.

Sports air filters offer little advantage over originals. This one is in the engine bay and so breathes in hot air, potentially reducing power.

The standard paper filter maximum flow ability steadily drops as the mileage steadily increases. The reason is simple: the standard filter is filtering, becoming blocked with the tiny particles that may otherwise slowly erode the engine. A sports air filter does not become so readily blocked, usually because it has let through the harmful particles.

Don't be too quick to condemn sports filters, though. Filters that use oil actually catch particles as the air infiltrates the sponge, and as long as they are washed out and re-oiled as per the manufacturer's instructions, they can work very well.

The other thing to bear in mind is that the stock filter is designed to help the engine last for well over 100,000 miles. If you rebuild the engine every year to keep it sweet for racing, this level of filtration is irrelevant. Indeed, some racers don't use a filter at all, but this is dangerous because of the risk of breathing in debris from the track – and what happens when the car inevitably visits the gravel trap?

For a fast road car, simply replacing the stock paper filter every year should maintain peak performance in most environments. If you use the car in dusty or sandy conditions, more frequent changes are required, and the paper filter is very good at catching the highly abrasive particles in sand.

Simply fitting a performance filter without any other engine modifications

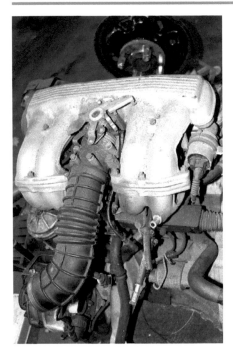

The standard M40 intake is also well designed, with long runners to promote a good spread of torque.

will not produce any more power than if it had a new standard filter. Some people believe they get more power, simply because the old standard filter was blocked, and the new performance filter has merely restored power to the standard level.

Noise

The stock intake is also designed to reduce noise. The filter element is quite absorptive, and the ram tube also helps to stop the noise escaping the airbox. A performance intake system can release more of the engine's natural induction roar, which can be quite pleasing, and if nothing else makes the car sound faster!

Airflow meter

The next obstruction on most E30s is the airflow meter. The L Jetroninc 'Flapper' meter is not great on tuned engines. Larger variants are available from cars like period Jaguars, and require a suitable adjustment of the ECU to work.

It is also possible to use a highly

modified ECU or use a mappable ECU to eliminate the airflow meter completely, see section 4-11 for more details.

COOLING SYSTEM

The internal combustion engine is not very efficient. Only about 30% of the heat energy from the fuel gets turned into usable power, another 30% goes straight into the cooling system, and the rest of the heat disperses through the exhaust, noise and vibration. What that means is: if you double the power output of the engine, you also have to double the heat rejection performance of the cooling system.

There are two critical aspects. First, getting the heat out of the engine metal and into the coolant and oil. Second, getting the heat out of the coolant and oil into the air. It is very important to understand this – it's not as straightforward as it sounds.

This picture gives some idea how much space there is for cooling. As standard, the radiator is behind the bodywork, but with a little imagination there is space to mount a radiator further forward.

Engineering the coolant

Inside the engine is a given surface area – not a lot we can do about that, so the only way of getting more heat transferred is to make the coolant

colder, or modify it so that it accepts the heat faster. One way is to use a 'Water Wetter' fluid. This breaks down the surface tension layer between the coolant and the metal, increasing the heat flow. It is not a massive difference, but on one of my race cars it reduced coolant temperature by nearly 10°C during a hot race, and let me run a little more advance. The downside is it does not work on glycol, so you have to reduce antifreeze content to about 10%, and it has poorer corrosion protection properties. So, it's no use for cold climates or a road car in the winter, plus it needs changing more often depending on use – possibly twice a year – but for race cars it is a useful tool.

Water is a better coolant than antifreeze, not by a huge amount, but it does make a difference on a race or track car. But 10% is about the minimum concentration, otherwise you risk high corrosion rates.

For a road car, it goes the other way. The blend of alloy and iron on E30 engines means there is always a danger of electrolytic corrosion. I run my road cars at 50% water/antifreeze all year, and change it every two years before it goes acidic.

The space in front of a standard radiator is big enough for extra oil coolers, intercooler, and an electric fan.

Oil coolers

All cars have oil cooling, even the base models without an oil cooler. The sump acts as a cooling system with heat passing through the metal into the engine bay air. If you don't have an oil

Standard radiator options. On the left is the neat M40 radiator with integrated expansion tank; on the right is the 325i radiator with oil cooler.

cooler and you tune the engine, you need to maintain healthy airflow round the sump.

As the engine power exceeds about 100bhp, sump cooling becomes inadequate on an E30, so an additional oil cooler is fitted on high-power models. This is a reasonable size for up to about 200bhp – above that and a larger cooler is a good idea

The oil cooler should keep the oil temperature in the sump between 80 and 110ºC. This is hot enough to get rid of any moisture and fuel that escapes past the piston rings and keeps the oil in good condition. Modern engine oils can run at higher temperatures, but over 130ºC is usually bad as the oil starts to decompose and get very thin.

Running a large cooler on a road car can give problems with over-cooling when the car is not being driven flat out. In this case, an oil thermostat can increase oil life, reducing drag on the engine from thick cold oil.

Radiators
The size of radiator needs depends heavily on the intended use and the airflow through it, which is absolutely

critical. Race cars that are always at speed often have no fans, or just a small one for when they come into the pits, whereas a family car expected to tow a caravan in heavy traffic will need a substantial engine-driven fan to get reasonable airflow at low engine

speeds. For this reason, you cannot say something like 'the standard radiator is good for 200bhp.' A 900bhp F1 race car will have smaller radiators than a 120bhp family Saloon car!

So, before changing the radiator size, first check the airflow is right. Crucially, check that the hot air from the back of the radiator has a way of escaping the engine bay, otherwise it will back up and reduce airflow and cooling capacity. If the engine bay is full of V12, maybe a few small vents in the bonnet are needed.

The E30 came with two main radiator sizes: the 4- and 6-cylinder variants. The smaller unit had an integrated header tank at the side, which frees space in the engine bay. The larger unit has approximately 20% more frontal area for cooling.

For a higher capacity unit, the E28 535i radiator is a popular choice, and fits directly in 6-cylinder E30 shells.

Checks
Before doing any performance tuning, check the cooling system is in good order, replace any perished hoses and leaking gaskets, and flush the system

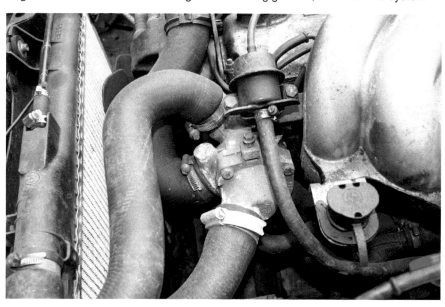

Keeping the system in good condition is vital. Replace perished hoses, check for cracks around the hose clips, and corrosion on the aluminium castings.

if possible. Thoroughly inspect the radiator for corrosion or damage, and repair if necessary.

If the car overheats in normal use, there is a fault that must be rectified. Using a fan as a 'sticking plaster' will only mask the problem, and it may get worse.

Electric fans

The cooling fan has a very important job to do. The radiator passes heat from the coolant into the surrounding air, which has to be replaced constantly for the system to work. On most cars, when travelling faster than around 20mph, the natural airflow through the engine bay should do the job. (In fact, that's why some race cars don't have fans at all.) But in traffic or when idling, there is no natural airflow, and a fan is needed to prevent overheating.

That said, certain cars need a fan at speed, too – some crowded engine bays, such as an E30 with a V12 in, cause the air to stall due to under-bonnet pressure build-up at speed, so on these cars the radiator requires a fan.

Fan technology has advanced significantly over the last 30 years.

Blades are now set at asymmetric spacings to break up the noise pattern, curved to reduce the noise from the leading edge as it cuts through the air, and twisted to improve efficiency. Motor technology has marched ahead, too. The traditional problem with electric fans was that the motor obscured a lot of the airflow, but modern materials have made motors smaller and more powerful. Remember, the E30 came out in 1981, which means parts such as the fans were designed in the '70s!

Visco drive engine-driven fans

A solid engine-driven fan is running all the time, whether or not the extra cooling is needed. This is moderated by the E30 visco unit, which should decouple the fan when the engine is cold, allowing the fan to freewheel, but gradually engage as the temperature rises. The visco unit also limits fan speed by restricting how much torque can be transmitted, which saves some power and improves fuel economy. With older cars these units may have failed, often seizing up and becoming solid, and replacement parts can be difficult to find, as well as pricey.

For the visco drive fan to draw enough air at idle it has to be very big, which makes it draw far too much air when the engine is at speed. Often several kilowatts of power will be wasted. In comparison, the electric fan, triggered by a temperature switch, only operates when needed, which saves on fuel. The great advantage is that this give full airflow when the engine is idling, theoretically making overheating in traffic a thing of the past, and on a racetrack they are essential when coming into the pits after a race.

Replacing an engine driven fan with an electric one

Usually an electric fan will replace the existing mechanical fan, so it needs to be sized to provide the same performance, unless it is to augment cooling for heavy towing work, in which case it can be smaller. Fan manufacturers can advise the best option for your car.

When the existing mechanical fan is removed, the bolts that attach the pulley to the water pump must be replaced with shorter ones, or washers used to pack the bolts out to the original depth.

There is some debate as to the best method of mounting the fan. Radiator manufacturers say avoid mounting the fan directly onto the radiator core – the tubes were never designed to hold the weight, and although some older designs may just about cope, it's best to use a separate mounting frame and preserve the radiator. But fan manufacturers counter by pointing out that there are almost no reports of failure, and the few of those there are turn out to be due to corroded radiators or incorrect fitting.

The fan must be as close as possible to the radiator. Any gap would let air escape, taking an easier route away from the radiator. However, the fan must not strike the radiator – bear in mind that it will move slightly as the car hits bumps in the road.

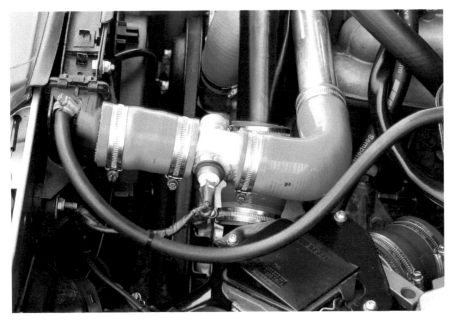

Adaptor tubes like this are ideal for mounting a thermo-switch to control an electric fan.

Shrouds help ensure the air to/from the fan has to pass through the radiator core. On some cars with an existing shroud, it may be possible to mount an electric fan directly to it.

Connect the fuse to the battery – never draw the supply voltage by cutting into an existing circuit, as this will overload it.

If using a kit with a controller, follow the manufacturers directions to hook up all the parts. Usually this is very simple, and may only require one more wire from the switch to the fan. If making your own control, you will need to either fit a temperature switch into the cooling pipes, or use an electronic control unit linked to the temperature sensor.

Ensure the earth from the fan is connected to sound bodywork.

To adjust the fan, allow the engine to warm up. Keep a close eye on temperature – as it gets to normal, the fan should come on, then the temperature should fall slightly and the fan switch off. If the fan doesn't come on when expected, try adjusting the control to a lower temperature until the fan operates. If the temperature goes significantly above normal without the fan coming on, switch off immediately and investigate the fault. Never allow the temperature to get into the red.

Warning!
In most systems the fan is permanently live, so could come on briefly after the engine is switched off. Avoid contact with the fan unless the system is made safe.

FUEL-INJECTION SYSTEM
The standard E30 fuel-injection system has gone through many revisions over the model's life, but has always provided good performance and has some tuning potential. These days,

The standard fuel-injection system can cope with modest improvements in power, but needs to be in good condition.

there are so many ECU and fuel system options that it can be tempting to depart from the standard system altogether, but with a few changes, stock parts can be quite useful.

Mapping
Fitting a new tune to an otherwise standard engine will never make a huge difference – if there is no more air going in, you are not really going to get any more power out.

Having said that, the standard tune does make some compromises, and tuning them out can make the car feel a little more lively. At the top end, most standard E30 engines run rich. This is to keep combustion chamber temperatures under control in the harshest of likely environments, such as towing a big trailer up a steep hill in Arizona (which is actually one of the tests BMW does). This over-fuelling goes slightly beyond the rich point for peak power, so making it a bit leaner can give up to 10bhp more, and as long as you leave the heavy trailer at home when driving up long steep hills in a desert, you might avoid engine damage.

Non-catalyst cars run slightly lean at part load to improve fuel economy. By enriching slightly under these conditions, the throttle response feels

For race and highly modified engines a rolling road session is essential to ensure fuelling and ignition timing is correct throughout the rev and load range.

faster and the engine seems more willing, although if you took it on a racetrack there would be no difference because full load is identical.

In summary, a chip tune on a standard engine will not transform it into a race winning monster, but it can make it feel nicer to drive, so for a road car it can be a good option. However, stick to the well-known tuning companies – some 'have a go' types just dial in loads more fuel everywhere, resulting in washed bores, engine wear, and poor performance. Beware of internet bargains.

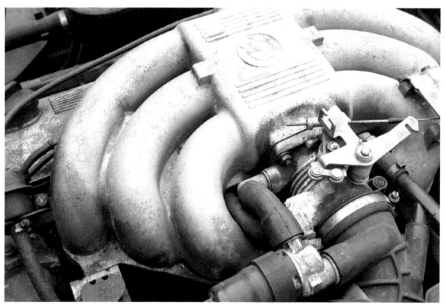

The idle valve can gum up, making the engine prone to stalling. Removing and cleaning with WD40 can revive it.

The biggest cause of problems with old fuel-injection systems are the connectors. Vibration loosens the contact's grip, and tarnishing increases resistance.

Once the engine is mechanically modified, remapping the ECU becomes a lot more important. Whilst the standard system can cope with small changes in performance, once the airflow exceeds production limits the fuel and spark will be inadequate. The Motronic system was quite advanced for its time, and can be remapped by specialists with good results, although with the age of the electronic circuits approaching a quarter century, you might want to consider the potentially more reliable option of a modern ECU.

Mappable ECUs allow the engine to be tuned exactly to suit the setup you are running. To make sure you have the right fuel and spark under all conditions, you need to get the car on a rolling road dynamometer, or take the engine to an engine dynamometer.

One halfway house is the 'piggy back' ECU: a small computer wired between the standard ECU and the sensors and actuators. It reads the signals and adjusts them to cope with engine modifications. The system is mapped in a similar way to a standalone ECU, but because the standard ECU is doing a lot of the hard work it can be made a lot cheaper.

Injector and fuel pump sizing

A petrol flow of 1.37cc/min has an energy flow equivalent to 1bhp, but engines are less than 30% efficient and

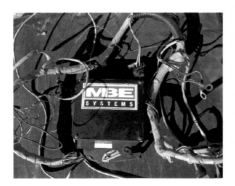

For heavily modified engines, it may work out easier and cheaper to change to a mappable ECU, such as this MBE941.

need a safety margin to allow for full load enrichment, so in reality you should aim for 5cc/min per bhp.

Ideally, fuel injectors at max power

will still be running at less than 100%. Most manufacturers aim for closer to 80%, so once you calculate your maximum fuel needs, add a safety margin of about 20%.

Similarly, it is wise to over-spec the fuel pump as well to cope with an aged fuel filter, etc. The universal Bosch in-line fuel pump 0-580-254-044 flows 4400cc/min at 3 bar – enough for over 400bhp.

Below are some injector values for E30 standard engines. I've indicated a potential bhp figure for both four- and six-injector configurations, to give an idea of the swap potential. This assumes 30% thermal efficiency and a duty cycle of 80%, so potentially you could get a bit more. These are all at 3 bar fuel pressure, so the figure could be improved with more pressure, too.

Application (E30)	Engine type	Part number	cc/min	Bhp 4-cyl	Bhp 6-cyl
316, 318, 325i	M40, M20	0-280-150-715	152.4	122	183
318	M10	0-280-150-211	147.1	118	177
318is	M42	0-280-150-714	213.9	171	257
2.7eta	M20	0-280-150-126	191.8	154	230
M3	S14	0-280-150-201	258.0	207	310

Injector values for E30 standard engines. The old Bosch 0-280-150-126 injectors have been superseded by 0-280-150-160, which have the same characteristics.

The fuel pump, filter and pulse damper are under the car, and suffer badly from corrosion. Check and replace as necessary.

There is a fair amount of tuning that can be done with the standard ECU and air meter.

A rising rate fuel pressure regulator can help tune the standard system by increasing fuelling at high loads.

When swapping injectors, there are a few things to bear in mind. First, the seals will have bonded firmly to the fuel rail if they are original. Removing the fuel rail may take some considerable force. The rail is full of fuel, and if the car ran recently it could still be under pressure, so there is a huge risk of flinging fuel into your eyes and all around the engine bay. Wear fuel proof gloves and goggles for this bit, and make sure the battery is disconnected – you don't want any accidental sparks!

There may be light corrosion above the lower O-ring on the manifold, and below the upper O-ring on the fuel rail. Also, bits of perished O-ring may remain when extracting the old ones. All this must be cleaned up before fitting new seals. Injectors use very small holes to squirt fuel in a nice fine mist, and any debris floating into the injector will ruin your day. Also, any surface roughness around the O-ring seats can compromise sealing, so it is vital to clean them and make sure no debris is in the fuel rail before reassembling.

The fuel rail can be manoeuvred forward to remove, but accessing the injector seats in the manifold is a bit more tricky, particularly the ones obscured by the intake manifold curving round on top of them. When removing the old injectors, to stop loose debris falling into the engine I use an air line, and try to dislodge flaky bits with a wire brush before taking anything apart. Then I give the seals a spray with WD40 to ease them on their way out and bind any remaining dust, so it doesn't fall in.

When installing new injectors, use new O-rings and lubricate them with a little engine oil so that they can move into the fuel rail and manifold recesses easily, and seat properly.

When it's all back together, remember the fuel rail will be empty. To fill it you can keep turning on the ignition for three-second bursts without starting the engine; the fuel pump will run for a few seconds each time to prime the system. Even so, the air will still be in there, so the engine may take a while to fire up, and may cough a few times before settling down.

Air meter tuning

Back in the day it was quite common to tweak the performance of an L-Jetronic

The standard air meters can be adjusted, but this rarely gives a completely satisfactory result. Larger units can also be fitted.

system by opening the lid on the airflow meter, often referred to as the 'flapper,' and clicking round the spring retention wheel to relieve tension. For a given airflow the flap moves further, telling the ECU that more air is flowing, and causing the engine to run richer. The problem is that the meter only affects fuelling up to about half throttle and mid revs – above this, the fuelling is based mainly on throttle position and rpm. Whilst this can make light throttle feel a little more lively, it will not affect full load fuelling, so if the engine has been modified to flow more air it will still run lean at full load, with potentially disastrous results.

Early airflow meters did create a small reduction in flow. One way round this is to use a bigger unit from another car, such as a Jaguar of the same era, and then tune the ECU to suit.

Another solution is to remove the meter altogether and modify the ECU to run purely off throttle position and engine speed. This is a big tear up of the ECU, and it may work out better and cheaper to fit a modern mappable ECU instead.

Throttle body injection systems

These look like a set of sidedraught carburettors, and sound pretty much the same too! With a short intake run, the power band is pushed up the rev range. They suit race engines with the right cams and potentially higher compression ratios. They also need an airbox with a suitable cold air intake, otherwise they will be sucking on hot air from the engine bay.

Fuel pump, tank and filter

On a race car, the lateral G forces are high enough to cause the fuel to move to the side of the standard fuel tank and starve the fuel pump. There are two main ways round this.

The first is to use baffles or a special sponge in the tank to slow the movement of fuel; after all, corners don't

For highly modified engines, it is often simpler to remove the airflow meter and map a new ECU based on manifold pressure or throttle position instead.

last more than a few seconds, so this does the job.

The other way is to use the conventional pump to feed a small separate reservoir of about one litre, called a swirl pot, which in turn feeds the primary fuel pump. This works very well indeed, and is particularly useful on rally cars, which bounce all over the place.

Fuel coolers

Fuel in the engine fuel rail absorbs a fair amount of heat. As excess fuel is recirculated to the tank, the fuel heats up. Hot fuel is more prone to vapour locks on hot restarts, and the lower density reduces power. So, a return line fuel cooler can be used to ease this problem.

GEARBOX

Many gearboxes were used in the E30. There were sports gearbox options with close ratios, economy versions with wider ratios, weak ones and strong ones, and if the E30 range doesn't suit your application, there is also a number of relatively simple swap options from other BMW models, including 6-speed boxes. If you can't find the right box, you're not looking hard enough!

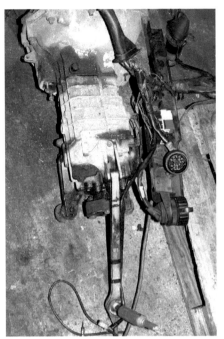

BMW gearbox identification can be tricky. Even the part number on the side can be misleading.

Many people swap their gearbox due to it failing after a few track events, but often this is because the box was worn in the first place, or the oil overheated. These cars are all quite old now, so expecting a stock gearbox to be in a condition suitable for motorsport is a bit optimistic – at the very least change the oil, but if the car is doing serious competition work it is worth spending a few hours stripping the box and rebuilding it with new bearings, and replacing anything that's worn. For long races it may be worth fitting a gearbox oil cooler, too.

The torque limit for these gearboxes depends on use. Basically, the size of the cogs dictates the maximum torque they can handle before braking, but if the gearbox is used in motorsport it will get hot, and at extremes the oil doesn't work as well and the gearbox will wear faster. As an example, the practical torque limit for a Getrag 240 for motorsport applications is in the region of 250lb-ft, but for a road car it might cope with 300lb-ft, or even more for very short periods.

The 260/265 Series are bigger, and bigger cogs are obviously stronger. These boxes were even used on Jaguar V12s briefly. Tuners have successfully used them with engines producing over 400lb-ft, but the downside is that they are also heavier. There is no point fitting a box with a capacity far higher than your engine output, and dragging the extra weight about for no reason.

Amazingly, the 260 was very long-lived. Applications include the Holden Commodore (1996-2004) and the Cadillac CTS (2002-2005), which means there are some relatively new secondhand boxes about and a good supply of spare parts.

There is some cross fertilisation in these Getrag gearboxes. The overdrive 265/6 and the close ratio 'dog-leg' 265/5 both use the same casing as the earlier 4-speed 262, but with an extra section bolted in, so the casings are marked '262,' which can cause some confusion. They all use the basic gear set, but with different cogs to the 260.

The 262 and 265 have removable bell-housings allowing a degree of

swapping, but the 260 and 240 have an integral bell-housing, so you will need one that matches your engine bolt pattern.

If swapping BMW gearboxes, the final thing to bear in mind is that the 4- and 6-cylinder cars have a difference of 10 degrees in the engine angle, so if you turbo your M10 and put a 260 behind it, you will need to modify the mounts and gear linkages slightly.

The E36 had a selection of gearboxes that may be of use. A Getrag 250, the ZFS5D310Z and ZF S5D320Z were used on the M3, with the three digit number giving an approximate indication of the maximum torque limit in Nm. An E36 323i clutch bearing will work with an M20 flywheel and the ZF E36 gearbox. The E36 ZF box is about 50mm longer than a Getrag 260, with a different output flange to an E30; the 328 E36 propshaft should sort this out.

The Getrag 240/5 gearbox from a 318is (M42, '88-'90) is often used on M50 engine swaps, as it bolts straight on and has a wider spread of gears than the M50 gearbox.

Gearbox options for V8 conversions usually centre around

gearboxes originally fitted to the V8. The M60 V8 came with either a 5- or 6-speed manual, plus ZF autos. The 5-speed is roughly similar to the gearbox used on the M3 E30, and an M3 propshaft allegedly fits.

The 6-speed is 120mm longer and has a larger output flange, so a custom prop is in order, with the back end matching the E30 diff and the front matching the gearbox. Possible donors include the E34 540i.

The 6-speed is also wider than an E30 gearbox, but some people remove one side of the crossmember and fabricate new parts, so the gearbox fits without transmission tunnel modification.

Gear oil

The synchro mechanism is dependent on friction to work properly, so it is very sensitive to the friction characteristic of the gear oil. Automatic gearbox fluid has friction modifier to help the clutch packs in an auto to grip well. This can also help the synchro hubs grip in a manual gearbox, and potentially speed up gear changes. BMW actually specified Dextron II ATF in the Getrag 260 manual gearbox used in the E34.

For reference, the viscosity of gear oils uses a different scale to engine oil, but an 80W gear oil is about the same viscosity as a 30W engine oil, as well as Dextron II ATF.

Autos

Most performance tuning involves the manual gearboxes, but I want to

Problem areas can include the gearbox mounts and the propshaft coupling.

To give you an idea of the different prop lengths available, the top one is from a 325i and the lower one from a 316i.

The different styles of centre bearing: top is from a post-face-lift model, and the lower one from a pre-face-lift model.

briefly mention the automatics. There are two areas where an auto has some advantages: rallying, and drag racing, because full-power upshifts are possible, which can save half a second each time a gear change is required. Also, on very muddy rally stages full power downshifts can prevent loss of forward momentum. If the car has been modified with a modern V8 or V12, using the 5- or 6-speed auto with a replacement performance gearbox controller, such as Compushift, allows a paddle shift option, making it a serious trackday option. On older, non-electronic boxes, the hydraulic control can be locked for full manual control. However, usually the extra weight and less favourable gear ratios make it a poor choice for most types of circuit racing.

Below are some gearbox specifications.

GEARSTICK

One of the criticisms of the E30 is that sometimes the gear selector mechanism has a long throw and can become sloppy, making it difficult to change gear quickly and accurately, particularly in racing conditions.

In its original condition, the mechanism is actually reasonably good. It offers good vibration isolation, which prevents noise and vibration from being transmitted into the bodyshell, making for a more relaxing drive. This is achieved by mounting the gearstick on an extension bar bolted to the gearbox with soft rubber isolators, and supporting the back end with a large soft rubber bush mounted to the transmission tunnel behind the gearstick, so that little of the engine vibration is connected to the shell. This is further enhanced by isolating rubber bushes and an isolating collar on the gearstick shaft. But all this isolation introduces a slight vagueness to the selection mechanism – not a problem for normal road use if in good condition, but it can be a bit awkward in the heat of a race.

Another criticism is that the gearstick has a relatively long travel,

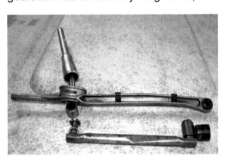

A typical standard gear linkage. The top steady bar is mounted on isolation rubbers at each end. The gear stick is also isolated and sits in a cup with plastic bearings that wear.

Model	Code	Year	Type	1st	2nd	3rd	4th	5th	Reverse
316i, 318i, 320i, 324d	E30	1988-1994	Getrag240	3.72	2.02	1.32	1.00	0.81	3.45
325i, 325ix, 324td	E30	1988-1994	Getrag260	3.83	2.20	1.40	1.00	0.81	3.46
325i, 325ixSports	E30	1988-1994	Getrag265	3.35	2.03	1.36	1.00	0.81	3.18
M3 (US)	E30	1986-1992	Getrag265/6	3.38	2.20	1.40	1.00	0.81	3.46
M3 (Euro)	E30	1987-1992	Getrag265/5	3.72	2.40	1.77	1.26	1.00	4.23
M3 Group A2.3 and 2.5	E30		Getrag265/5	2.34	1.68	1.36	1.15	1.00	2.66
316, 318i	E30	1982-1983	ZFS5-16	3.72	2.20	1.40	1.00	0.81	3.46
318is	E30	1989-1990	Getrag240/5	3.73	2.02	1.32	1.00	0.81	3.45
318is	E30	1990-1991	GetragS5D200G	4.23	2.52	1.66	1.22	1.00	4.04
533i, 633csi, 733i	Various	1983-1984	Getrag260	3.83	2.20	1.40	1.00	0.81	3.46
325e, 528e	E34	1983on	Getrag260	3.83	2.20	1.40	1.00	0.81	3.71
328i, M3	E36	1992-1998	ZFS5D310Z	4.2	2.49	1.66	1.24	1	2.93/3.23
318i, 323i, 325i	E36	1992-1999	ZFS5D310Z	4.23	2.52	1.66	1.22	1	2.93/3.23
M3	E36	1995-1999	ZFS5D320Z	4.2	2.49	1.66	1.24	1	2.93/3.23

E30 gearbox specifications.

again making fast gear changes a little more difficult. This was addressed in the Z3, which uses basically the same system, but with the pivot points moved to reduce travel. This can be a nice modification on an E30, although parts are getting harder to find.

Rebuilding the links

If the rubber bushes have perished, replacing them with good quality standard items will obviously help, but one of the most common areas for wear is the ball joint at the base of the gearstick. This sits in a cup in the extension rod, and is held in with a plastic retainer ring. This retaining ring wears and can become brittle and break up, which makes it very difficult to select gears accurately. Unfortunately, replacement rings are becoming scarce, although repair kits are still available, and the chances are that even secondhand selector mechanisms will be worn, too.

Some people replace the extension rod front bush with a solid aluminium

or nylon item. This removes a lot of the side-to-side play and puts more strain on the mounting area, so it is very important that the rear mounting into the transmission tunnel is still soft enough to cope with the movement of the engine/gearbox in use. The link rod bush can again be replaced with a solid unit. Finally, the gearstick can be cut down for reduced throw.

Solid links

For motorsport applications, it is in some ways easier to just make a new mechanism using spherical (rose type) joints.

The extension rod has to be bolted solidly to the gearbox to prevent the rear end wobbling. The standard rod uses a soft locating bush mounted to the transmission tunnel, which cannot be used with a solid extension rod due to gearbox and engine movement when running. This puts a lot of stress on the gearbox mounts, so a brace must be used to spread the load safely and steady the rod sufficiently.

The raw ingredients for the new linkage: threaded rod, spherical joint, box section steel, and some packing pieces.

The original link rod can be used, replacing the rear bush with a solid item. A new gearstick can be machined from rod, or as a cheaper alternative, a length of threaded rod (studding) can be used. If using threaded rod, bear in mind that the threads weaken it, and that it will be feeling the full force of a competitive driver, so it has to be reinforced by slipping over some tube cut to length.

The way I went about this was by copying the length and mounting positions of the original gearstick, then adjusting the position of the spherical joint until I got the throw and feel that suited my driving style. Next I removed the gearstick again, fitted a packing washer between the spherical joint and the lower mounting so there was no play between them, then cut a length of tube to cover the threaded rod between the spherical joint and the gear knob. Once the retaining nut was tightened, the tube was compressed and took the side loading, leaving the threaded rod just in tension with no bending force applied. I used the sort of threaded rod where the thread had been formed by rolling – this makes the root of the thread a nice curve. Cheaper threaded rod has the thread cut into it which can leave a sharp angle at the thread root which weakens it considerably.

Control location

When doing any of these modifications it is important to keep the gear knob in

Building a custom link system with spherical (rose-type) joints.

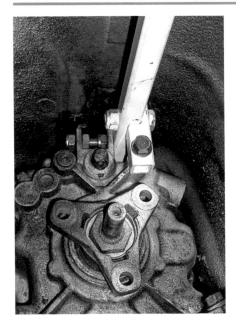

The new top link rigidly bolted to the gearbox: note the extra vertical bracing piece.

The E30 diff sits in a crossmember that also holds the semi-trailing arms. The diff is a stressed member, and its rear mounting prevents the crossmember from tilting.

the right position, if it ends up too low then it will be uncomfortable to operate and mistakes become more likely.

When building a race car, the usual sequence of events is to locate the race seat where it needs to be, then move the controls, including the gear knob, so that they sit in the ideal location for a particular driver. The more naturally the controls fall to hand, the easier they are to operate.

DIFFERENTIAL

The E30 came with one of two differential casings. Within the BMW community, these are referred to as the 'small case' for most of the smaller engines, and the 'medium case' for the larger engines. As you might have guessed, these two have different sized cases and contain different sized parts – the 'small' unit has the advantage of being a few kilos lighter, which suits 4-cylinder cars and racers keen to keep the weight down, but is not really suitable for sustained use with engines over about 200bhp. However, this depends on a number of other factors,

too. As with gearboxes, there are two limiting factors in differential selection: firstly, the teeth on the crown wheel and pinion have a torque limit, so to some extent the type of differential needed depends on which gearbox is used and the ratios, particularly first. The second limiting factor is the heat generated when running at high loads. The small unit can cope with high power for shorter periods than the medium sized unit. Luckily the two units are interchangeable and use the same mounting points on the crossmember and body, so if you are modifying a small-engined car for high outputs, it is a reasonably straightforward job to swap to the medium unit. However, the small diff needs slightly longer half-shafts than the wider medium diff. With the car up on stands and the suspension at full droop it is easy to fit a medium diff with small diff half-shafts, but as the suspension loads up the shafts are compressed and the limit of travel in the CV joints is reached, eventually the CVs would fail or the diff casing would crack.

So the rule is simple; if using a medium case diff then you must use medium case half-shafts. If using a small case diff you must use the small case half-shafts.

Also, the half-shafts are different between the drum- and disc-braked models, and between ABS models, which have the speed sensor ring gear

The 'small' diff found at the back of most 4-cylinder models.

on the CV end, and non-ABS models, which don't.

In case you are wondering, there is a 'large case' differential too, although not usually fitted on the E30. The large differential is found behind the large-six engined BMWs of that era, such as the 635/535 etc. It has a slightly different mounting system, so is not a straight swap, but as ever it can be done, and was used by BMW South Africa in its 333.

Identification

To quickly identify which case it is, the small case has six bolts holding the rear cover on, the medium case has eight bolts.

There should be a metal tag held on by one of the rear cover bolts. This will have the ratio stamped on it. BMW LSD units have a large 'S' stamped on the tag, and sometimes also appear in white paint on the top of the casing.

Ratios

A variety of ratios was available in the E30 range, with taller gearing for economy models and lower gearing for sports models. The differentials were used across the BMW range. For instance, the medium case unit can also be found on cars such as the E28 or E24, providing a greater potential source of used parts. However these units have a different rear cover and rear mounting, so you would need an E30 rear cover to bolt on. Also E24/E28 half-shafts and output flanges have a different bolt pattern. Luckily, the output flanges can be swapped easily to the E30 items.

It is also possible to fit the internals from the later E36 and E34 differentials, including LSDs, into a medium case, but this requires some engineering skill to set up properly, so unless you know about crush washers and pre-loads, leave it to someone else.

Limiting slip

Some E30s had an LSD as standard, such as the 318is, and of course the M3. Also, the 6-cylinder Z3s, M-Sport Z3s, and M-Coupés have geared (Torsen type) LSDs. E24s, E28s, and E30s use clutch type LSDs, the small case using a single plate unit, and the medium case using a twin plate unit.

So, it is possible to find and install a secondhand unit, but beware: a damaged unit can be costly to repair, and it may work out cheaper to build a new LSD into your existing casing.

A number of companies such as Quaife offer LSDs for the E30.

The E30 plate-type LSD can be adjusted by changing the pre-load to suit the application, although setting up a diff needs careful measurement and some skill. However, for competition use it can be very helpful to change the locking characteristic – on very loose surfaces such as gravel and autocross circuits, some people set the LSD to be very stiff, or in extreme cases, locked

Model	318i/316	318i/is/316i	325/e/es	325i/is/iX	M3
Year	1982-87	1988-92	1984-87	1987-92	1987-91
Auto	3.91:1	N/A	2.78:1	2.91:1	N/A
Manual	3.91:1	4.10:1	2.78:1	3.73:1	4.10:1

E30 gear ratios.

The 'medium' diff found at the back of 6-cylinder models. (Courtesy Jim Cameron)

It's important to get the right halfshaft for the application. Although it's possible to fit the wrong ones, they can bind and damage the diff.

completely. A locked diff will force both rear wheels to turn at the same speed, which does tend to make the car go in a straight line. When cornering, one tyre will have to slip and traction can be reduced. On a race circuit, if the diff is too stiff the car will understeer going into corners, and oversteer coming out. It is all a matter of setting it up for the type of racing and the driver's style.

By comparison, the geared type of LSD used on later models directs more torque to the wheel with the most traction. Again, there is a pre-load that can be adjusted, but it is important to ensure there is always a minimum torque on either half-shaft – without this pre-load, if one wheel lost all traction there would be no cross-torque, and the LSD would allow that wheel to spin just like an open diff.

Rear bush

The rear mounting bush on the differential dictates how much the rear suspension crossmember rocks under load. For this reason, it should ideally be changed in conjunction with the crossmember bushes.

Cooling

If you look at the differential rear cover,

you will see some small cooling fins. In motorsport, preventing the differential oil from overheating is crucial if it is going to survive. For this reason, BMW developed another differential casing for the M Coupé which had much bigger cooling fins, basically forming a diff radiator that extends to the sides and about an inch below the differential. This cover can be fitted to normal medium differentials, too, but the lower edge can be a bit vulnerable on lowered cars.

For extreme motorsport applications, it is possible to remove the drain and fill plugs from the rear cover and connect an external oil cooler, either thermo-siphoning or using a small electric oil pump.

Oil

Differential oil is frequently overlooked, but is a crucial link in the reliability chain. If your diff melts, you're not going to win the race. Also, poor quality oil, or an incorrect quantity, gets hotter, taking power from the engine and reducing the power at the wheels by a small amount. If you are serious about winning, get serious about the oil that keeps it all together.

BMW specifies Hypoid 90 gear

oil for both open and LSD units, but plate type LSDs require oils with friction modifiers designed specifically.

BMW recommends SAF-XO for open diffs and SAF-XLS for plate type LSDs. Both are synthetic, so they have a very low level of impurities and last longer.

Avoid cheap oils. Stick to quality brands such as Castrol, Motul and Shell etc. Cheap oils are usually cheaper to make, because the process has less quality control and the oil may have more impurities.

SUSPENSION
Modifying the suspension on a car renowned for excellent handling may seem a bit challenging, and to be fair, the standard setup is pretty good when in proper working order. If your car doesn't handle well, the first thing to do is to check that nothing is broken or worn. Once that's done, there are several ways to modify the E30 suspension, depending on budget and intended use.

There is a very large number of suspension kits available for the E30. Some are very good, some are terrible,

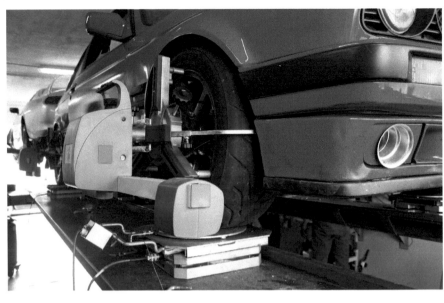

Setting up the suspension geometry can be complex with fully adjustable suspension, so some time spent with an expert and an accurate measurement system is vital. Here, geometry and corner weights are being set up. (Courtesy Jim Cameron)

but even a good one can ruin a car if the wrong specification is chosen.

There are two main suspension philosophies in the car world. Colin Chapman of Lotus fame recommended soft springs firmly damped, which allows the suspension to move and do its job whilst maintaining control. Many other companies including BMW go the other way, using harder springs to reduce body roll and suspension movement-induced camber change, but leave the damping a little softer to minimise the noise, vibration and harshness (NVH) transmitted into the car. Both ideas have merits, both have problems, so in the end it comes down to personal preference, even on a racing car where the handling has to match the driver's style in order to work as a package.

The starting point
Before modifying the suspension, get it checked on a laser alignment rig so you know where you are starting from. It may show up an underlying problem such as a bent linkage, or even an out-of-line chassis due to a crash. Fix any alignment issues before changing costly upgrade parts.

Another warning
Don't use cheap new parts available on certain internet sites. There is a

For the ultimate circuit racer, such as this M3 Touring Car, lower ride height and very high spring rates make sense. (Courtesy BMW)

Wheel bearings are another vital component, and, for race applications, a high temperature grease such as Castrol BNS may be needed.

A well set up E30 does not have to be extremely low. The front suspension works well when it can move up and down enough to respond to road irregularities. (Courtesy Jim Cameron)

The rear suspension experiences unhelpful camber change at very low ride heights. The E30 works well with the rear of the car slightly higher than the front. (Courtesy Jim Cameron)

large number of badly made parts about these days, and also a huge number of fake parts with correct part numbers and branding. If buying new suspension or brake parts, always buy from a reputable seller and buy a known brand such as BMW, Lemforder, Meyle or TRW. For example, there are cheap cast control arms about. There are huge forces on this part, so the real items are forged for strength. Unfortunately, the fake cast parts are often made from a mould taken from a real forged part, and so will have the distinctive forging line on the side. It is very difficult to distinguish between the fake and real parts, so your only protection is to buy from a good source. Fake parts can crack and catastrophically fail without warning.

Lowering

One of the first things to consider is ride height. Altering the front is reasonably straightforward, but the rear is a semi-trailing arm, and changing the ride height also changes the camber, toe and castor angles. What this means is that for most cars, dropping the ride height by up to about 40mm helps lower the centre of gravity and helps the car handle better on a racetrack, but dropping it much further will start to

reduce traction at the rear, as the wheel leans over too far and only uses the edge of the tyre.

For most road car applications, though, 40mm drop is fine, and in my opinion does make a positive improvement to the car's handling. But the higher spring rates of lowering kits will make the ride harsher on rougher roads, and of course there will be 40mm less ground clearance when negotiating potholes and speed bumps.

For race or extreme modified cars, going lower needs some adjustment of the rear swing arms to get the angles back to somewhere near correct.

Measure the wheel centre to arch height – this will be used as the datum point for all relative measurements and will help when setting adjustable ride height springs. Typical values are 380mm front and 400mm rear, standard on an early high rear arch car, so a 40mm lowered car might read 340mm front and 360mm rear.

The standard E30's rear is higher than the front. To check this, measure the distance from the sill to the ground at the front and rear edges. This difference allows for extra weight of rear passengers and luggage, but having a wedge-shaped space under the car with the low end at the front also improves high-speed stability, effectively working like a mild venturi and sucking the car

For simpler systems, it's useful to check the hub to arch height at each corner. This car measured 322mm front and 338mm rear, with a kit marked as '40mm lower.'

down. If your modifications result in the car being lower at the back than the front, then the opposite happens, and at speed a high-pressure wedge of air lifts the car, which is bad.

However low you go, always check there is adequate clearance for the tyre.

Softer suspension also works very well in wet conditions. If you fit adjustable suspension, adjust it! (Courtesy Jim Cameron)

Spring rates

There are two conflicting requirements for springs: the spring must be soft enough to allow the suspension to move readily over the undulations of the road, but it must also be stiff enough to minimise roll in corners and pitching when accelerating or braking. There is no perfect solution, and the best setup is again one that feels best to the driver.

Ultimately for a road car it becomes a matter of personal preference, but for track and race cars it depends on the circuit the car will run on. Very smooth tracks as used by F1 cars (such as Silverstone in the UK) favour hard springs for very high speed corners and minimal dive for hard braking, whereas rougher tracks as used in some club racing (Cadwell Park, Croft in the UK) with their lower speed corners favour softer springs to allow the wheel to move over the bumps. This softer spring and firmer damper idea seems to work very well on real back roads, too.

The springs are mounted

slightly inboard of the wheel, obviously, so the spring rate at the wheel is reduced by the lever action of the suspension. The struts at the front are angled so the spring force is pretty much what you get at the wheel, but the swing arm at the back has the spring halfway to the pivot point, so the springs have to be a lot stiffer than the

desired rate at the wheel. So where is a good starting point? Taking the rate at the wheel, as a general rule for cars like these a firm road spring rate at the front might be 160lb-in, a sportier road spring maybe 200lb-in, and a club level race rate might be in the 300lb-in region. Touring cars have been known to go as high as 600lb-in.

Rear spring rates are always lower, particularly in relatively light rear-wheel drive cars like these. Making the back too stiff will result in low traction and heavy oversteer. A fair starting point is to make the rear wheel rate half the front

Allowing the car to move on the suspension makes breakaway more progressive and the car more fun to drive on the limit, but does not give ultimate grip on a very smooth circuit. (Lee Marshall)

rate, but on a stripped-out racer it may be even less. A typical club race setup is about 100lb-in rear and 300lb-in front, but because of the lever action of the trailing arm the actual spring rate will need to be about 40% higher.

An everyday road car that may take rear passengers and luggage may work best with similar spring rates front and rear, as both axles will share the load more or less equally most of the time, but an all-out race car will need much softer rear springs than the front so as to balance traction in fast corners. The basic rule is the axle with the hardest springs has the least traction, so high-powered E30s can reduce the severity of the power on oversteer by having harder front springs.

The same goes for anti-roll bars – the harder they are, the less traction that axle will have in corners relative to the other one

An alternative to conventional road springs is to use standard race car springs, which are surprisingly cheap. They come in 2.25 or 1.9-inch diameters, and there is a very cheap way of making an ordinary front strut into a racing strut, by using a threaded tube that slips over the strut body and accepts adjustable spring platforms, allowing the ride height to be changed, but just as importantly it allows the corner weights to be balanced out, improving suspension performance.

Fitting race springs to the rear is a bit more tricky, as it requires converting to coilover dampers, which also requires modification of the rear arm and bodywork. The coilover unit can be fitted in place of the original damper if the mounting points are strengthened. Although the shock loading on the damper mounts can be higher than the static loading on the spring mounts, the combination of the two could potentially deform the standard mounting points.

Spring quality
To get a precise spring rate, the manufacturer has to use high quality steel and use exactly the right process. This all costs money, and is why decent springs can seem expensive. There are some very cheap spring kits available on the internet, but these are likely to be made with cheap steel and not heat-treated properly. This results in a high variation in actual spring rates – one kit I tested had rates that were up to 60% out from one side to the other. It can also result in the springs sagging over time.

Adjustable ride height
For racing, it is standard practice to have adjustable spring seats so that the ride height and corner weights can be fine-tuned. Usually this is done by using coilover damper units with a threaded sleeve that has a large locknut at the top of the spring. Direct replacement front struts are available in this form, but the rear would need converting from the standard spring location. This can be done by either strengthening the existing damper mounts on the trailing arm and body to take a coilover unit, or by welding on completely new mountings in the desired location. Another option is to fit an adjustable seat insert into the standard trailing arm spring mounting point. This is a short threaded tube that bolts into the hole at the centre of the spring seat. It also requires a shorter spring to allow for the height of the insert, so comes as part of a kit (such as the Bilstein PSS) containing the springs, adjustable seat and fittings.

Front struts can be bought pre-fitted with adjustable spring seats. Another option is to convert standard struts by using a threaded sleeve that slips over the strut tube and is welded on. If you go for one of these, first check the diameter of your strut tube – there are two sizes used on E30s. Most have the larger 51mm tube, but the pre-face-lift 4-cylinder models had the smaller 45mm strut.

Suspension modifications
The E30 suspension generally responds well to lowering. As well as dropping the centre of gravity, the rear arms increase camber as they go up, which can increase traction when powering out of corners, but going too far results in very high camber values, reducing traction for straight line acceleration or braking. This can be combated by cutting up the arm and re-welding it with the camber reduced to sensible values. Obviously this is a big job, but luckily some E30 specialists make exchange units that just bolt on. Unfortunately, this doesn't completely solve the traction problem on drastically lowered cars, because having the hub above the front pivot point of the arm means a tendency for the wheel to lift under acceleration. This can result in the axle hopping when doing a racing start, so some people also modify the arm and its mountings to raise the pivot points, which is quite a lot of work. The question you have to ask is: what does lowering the car so far achieve? If it is to get a specific look for a show car, then fine; but if it is for performance, lowering it a bit less may actually work better.

The front is slightly different. As the car is lowered, the lower wishbone tilts up at the wheel end. At the extreme it pulls the lower end of the strut inboard slightly, increasing positive camber, which in turn reduces cornering ability. Also, when braking heavily, particularly on a racetrack, as the front dives the camber gets even worse, and traction is reduced just as you need it the most, resulting in the brakes locking too easily. One way round this dive problem is to use anti-dive geometry by re-engineering the lower wishbone mounting points, either dropping the front or raising the rear. Another is to use very hard springs, but both options have their problems. A better solution is to introduce negative camber by using modified or adjustable lower wishbones to set the lower end of the strut further outboard. This also increases track width slightly, which can make a further small improvement to cornering, as well as making the car look a bit nicer.

Another option is to use modified or adjustable strut top mounts to pull the strut top inboard. This can be a better solution if you don't want to risk the tyre hitting the wheelarch at full bump.

Again, 40mm lower is generally viewed as optimum without a modified wishbone or strut top, but 60mm at the front coupled with 40mm at the back, so that it is slightly nose down, may improve downforce and stability at speed.

Fitting an adjustable spring and damper kit

First check the car is straight in the first place. Check the geometry using the string method or popper gauges. Then check the ride height as detailed in the 'Ride height' section.

Fitting the dampers and springs is as per the workshop manual, but I would fit new standard or harder race bushes to the dampers depending on application.

When fitting adjustable ride height springs, it is useful to set them to the desired height before fitting. They are

A coilover damper strut with an adjustable spring seat and spherical joint top mount. (Courtesy Jim Cameron)

This unit has a light 'helper' spring below the main spring to stop the latter dislodging at full droop. In normal use it is completely compressed. (Courtesy Jim Cameron)

usually quite slow to adjust in situ, so this saves a lot of time. If you know the corner weights of the car and the spring rate, you can work out the desired length – if the front corner weight is 500lb, and the spring is a 250lb-in item, it will compress by two inches when fitted.

If you don't know this information,

The rear suspension is very different: the spring is mounted inboard, so the lever action requires the spring rate to be much higher than the desired wheel rate. The beehive profile gives a rising rate effect. (Courtesy Jim Cameron)

This KW unit is independently adjustable for bump and rebound. The spring in the background is on an adjustable height bottom mounting. (Courtesy Jim Cameron)

it's trial and error. Basically, fit the springs and dampers, lower the car, take a measurement, jack up the car again to relieve the pressure on the spring seats, and adjust them by the difference between what you measured and what you wanted.

The threaded tube of adjustable spring mounts is prone to corroding, which, combined with the large nut diameter, can easily prevent adjustment in the future. To protect them, some people cover them with spray grease and for road or rally cars tie a plastic cover over the exposed portion. Other people apply a light coating of paint, thin enough to not interfere with the nut movement, or light enough to flake off when the nut is adjusted.

Roll

One area often overlooked is the anti-roll bars. The standard items are fairly soft, which is ideal for rougher roads where you really need the wheels to be independent. But once on a racetrack, the car will roll quite significantly. Lowering the car will reduce this, as will fitting harder springs, but a stiffer anti-roll bar set will reduce roll with less compromise of ride comfort on a road car, and allow slightly softer springs on

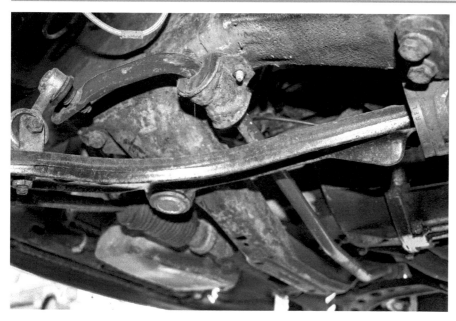

A good clubman's set-up, adjustable anti-roll bar with polyurethane bushes. The anti-roll bar bushes make a difference to how the initial roll motion is controlled.

The roll resistance is adjusted by bolting the drop link in one of the three possible mounting holes, changing the effective lever length.

a race car than would otherwise be the case, improving grip on rougher circuits.

Roll stiffness has a direct effect on grip. The stiffer the anti-roll bar, the less grip that axle has compared to the other one. This is one way of dialling in more or less oversteer on a race car: very stiff front and it will understeer, very stiff rear bar and you have oversteer – handy for a drift car.

Companies such as Eibach make adjustable anti-roll bars that allow you to adjust the handling to suit the circuit

and conditions – for instance, reducing oversteer for a wet race. I have known some racers to remove the rear anti-roll bar for wet races.

Front strut top mounts

The front strut top mounts can be moved by using either offset or adjustable top mounts to adjust camber, castor, and thus trail. BMW made offset top mounts to increase negative camber in the M3. It also made offset lower wishbone bushes, pulling the back of the wishbone outwards and so pushing

A race top mount that allows camber adjustment. (Courtesy Jim Cameron)

the wheel forwards. This increases castor and steering feel, as well as high-speed stability.

5-stud conversions

This is one of those areas that provokes intense argument. It all started with the E30 M3, which used modified 5 Series suspension parts that have wheels with five mounting bolts instead of the standard car's four.

The E30 M3 parts do bolt on to the standard car, and offer a slight increase in front brake disc size, wider track width, and slightly stiffer springs and dampers. The trouble is that very few were made all those years ago, so now the parts are rare and expensive. Also, the M3 front suspension puts the wheel further back, so M3 wings are also needed. This has driven many enthusiasts to try the more readily available E36 M3 parts instead, but there are some problems if the wrong parts are used.

The E36 parts do have the advantage of significantly bigger brakes than the E30 or E30 M3, but of course you could always fit a big brake kit to an E30 anyway. The danger is that more could be spent on a 5-bolt conversion than would be needed to convert E30 parts to the same performance level.

One point: the E30 M3 parts allow 15in wheels to be fitted, but the larger brake diameter and calliper position on the E36 requires a minimum of 16in wheels. However, there is a larger choice of wheels available for the 5-bolt pattern.

The E36 M3 had different front control arms and spindles to the normal E36. The control arm has the lower ball joint further forward to increase the kingpin inclination and improve high-speed stability. On its own, this would put the wheel too far forward, so the M3 also has spindles that move the wheel rearwards to compensate. Obviously if you end up with one of these items but not the other, the wheel will be in the wrong place and the geometry and handling will be very wrong.

The best bet is to take all the parts from an E36 M3, but if you have to get the bits separately you will need the following E36 M3 ('95 to '98) parts, also available from a Z3 M

Spindle/hubs, struts, brake discs and callipers with mountings (and ABS sensors if needed).

You will also need the control arms, but there was a change on the E36 M3, so ensure your items have the following part numbers: 31-12-2-228-461/462, or if from a Z3 M, 31-12-2-228-465/466, which are geometrically the same.

These also need the offset type of bushings to get everything to line up. The part numbers are E36 M3 31-12-2-228-461 (left) and 31-12-2-228-462 (right), or Z3 31-12-2-228-465 (left) and 31-12-2-228-466 (right)

The springs, strut tops and brake hoses will all be E30 items.

A word of warning: the struts corrode. It is vital to thoroughly check used items before buying them.

To convert the rear to 5-bolt, there are a few options. The simplest is to use the standard E30 trailing arms and fit hubs and brakes from an E36 or Z3. However, there are a few variations. Firstly, it depends on which trailing arm your E30 has. There were two bearing sizes: the lower power cars had a 72mm bearing, and the rest had the 75mm bearing that has been used for decades on other BMW and Porsche products. In both cases you will need the brake calliper from any E36, but the carrier from a 4-cylinder model (part number 34-21-1-162-436).

The smaller bearing was used on the 4-cylinder E36, and also the 4-cylinder Z3 models. The wheel bearing part number is 33-41-1-124-358, the hub number is 33-41-1-095-768 or 33-41-1-095-770, and the brake disc number is 34-21-6-758-552 or 34-21-1-164-399.

The larger bearing unit can be found on the Z3 6-cylinder models. The wheel bearing part number is 33-41-1-130-617, which is the same bearing as the standard E30, the hub number is 33-41-1-095-772, and the brake disc is 34-21-1-164-399.

If you need to replace the trailing arm anyway, another option is to fit the whole trailing arm with hub and brakes from a 4-cylinder E36 or Z3.

The downside of any of the above options is that the rear brake size is pretty much the same as before, so that's a lot of work just to have different wheels. To use larger brakes you could use the trailing arm from a Z3 M, which also has reinforcement at the weak points on the arm. Unfortunately, these are quite expensive and getting rarer. The hub also requires the Z3 M half-shafts and diff flanges, so it is a fairly big job, but it does use the same brakes as the E36 M3.

That makes it sound easy, but as ever there are complications, and here the big issue is track width. The 4-pot E36 hubs widen the track by 18mm each side, and the Z3 option is 23mm wider. To combat this, some people use E36/E46 staggered wheels. With a bit of work, fairly wide tyres can be fitted, such as a 245 on an ET41 or ET50 offset wheel. Or you could rework the wheelarches and possibly fit wider arches in the M3 style.

If you actually want to go wider still, you could use the Z3 trailing arm, which is a further 20mm each side. Add this to the 23mm extra in the hub, and compared to a standard E30 it adds 43mm each side.

Polyurethane bushes

The phrase 'poly bush' has become synonymous with any synthetic bushing material, a bit like the word Hoover is used for any vacuum cleaner, but more accurately it only refers to polyurethane, a soft plastic. The advantage over rubber is that it doesn't degrade over time so easily, and can be made in a variety of firmness to suit any application. And because they are firmer, they absorb less energy and run cooler. Typically, a poly bush will last between three (if it's getting hammered in a harsh environment) and ten (normal

The rear bush in the front lower wishbone is vital in controlling wheel movement: this polyurethane bush reduces unwanted movement.

road use) times longer than the rubber part.

Now, before talking any more about the magical properties of plastic, it's worth taking some time to put a word in for rubber. The reason it's used so much in the car industry is that it actually works very well and is cheap to make. Rubber is mixed with a variety of materials to get a precise firmness, and its shape is tailored to give the exact performance that the car requires. For instance, front control arm bushes have voids in so that they have less stiffness in one direction. It also has very good noise insulation properties, and is ideal for isolating road noise from the vehicle shell.

So why is it so often replaced? Well, this usually happens when the owner feels the car's handling has become sloppy or a bit soft, but this is usually because the rubber bushes are sufficiently old or worn that they no longer work as originally designed. In this situation, simply replacing the worn items with new rubber ones would restore the suspension's performance

Having said that, poly bushes can make a significant improvement to your car, as long as you choose the right type. Hard ones are best suited to high-performance vehicles, where minimal suspension compliance is beneficial

The usual measure of firmness is the Shore A scale. Most poly bushes are in the range of 70 (softest, quietest, often used for subframes) through 80 (often used for wishbone bushes and damper mounts) to 95 (firmest, used on coilover dampers and very high load areas). Different areas of the car require different firmness, depending on the magnitude of force applied, so when you buy a kit for a car it should contain a variety of hardness. All the bushes in a given kit will be dyed the same colour – this is the manufacturers way of denoting how sporty or comfy the overall kit is, not the individual Shore hardness of each bush.

The bush material, polyurethane, is made as a liquid and then poured into moulds. It is very important to have no bubbles in it when poured, otherwise the finished bush will be softer than intended, and can begin to disintegrate internally in use.

During manufacture, the material shrinks and the mould must be made to cope with this. The accuracy of the mould is critical, otherwise the bush may be impossible to fit.

There are several main differences between good bush kits and cheap bush kits. Even on some performance cars, there may be some bushes that need to move a fair amount. A good bush manufacturer will know this and tailor the design to suit. By comparison, the cheapest bushes on the market are often simply geometrical copies of the rubber item but made in polyurethane, which can work very badly in some situations.

It is sometimes tempting to just replace a few bushes with polyurethane as they wear out, but this can lead to imbalance in the car's handling. For instance, the differential rear mounting bush and the rear suspension crossmember bushes should be treated as a set, but things like front wishbone bushes can be treated in isolation with good effect.

Poly bushing the dampers means that as the car passes over a bump, the damper is immediately controlling the suspension movement, rather

than having to wait for the rubber to compress first. Although, to be fair, there is still some compliance in the poly bush, so it's not exactly black and white. The effect of this is that the wheel is a little more under control and grip is enhanced. Standard poly bushes will have no effect on refinement, but hard ones will transmit more road noise into the cabin.

There are two types of damper bush. In both cases they are a two-piece item looking like two top hats, either fitted on a shaft that goes through a hole the bodywork, or fitted into an eye with a cross bolt attaching it to the damper mounting.

When undoing the nut on a damper shaft, it is common for the shaft to start rotating. Most shafts have a very small flattened area at the end that you can get a special tool on. Many a swear word has issued forth when this tip shears off in the mouth of a set of mole grips, so first ensure penetrating oil has soaked into the nut, clear rust, and grot on any visible thread area and the shaft tip, then grip the tip securely with a tool that fits well. Never grip the shaft below the bush with anything metal, or you risk marking the shaft, which will damage the damper seal.

The shaft bushes usually have slightly dished retaining washers. Check all the metalwork is in good order with no rough patches. Renew them if they cannot be brought up to scratch.

The eye type of bushes usually provide much more opportunity to practise swearing. Often they are pressed in, and the rubber slowly bonds to the metal, unlike metalastic mounts where the rubber always seems to peel away from the metal just to annoy you. There is usually a steel tube insert in the middle where the bolt passes through. A good poly bush kit will come with replacement tubes, but if not, the original tube must be reclaimed and thoroughly cleaned or replaced.

Pressing the old bush out is best done in a press or at the work bench with a vice. One popular way is to use

two sockets, one bigger than the bush but small enough for the metal eye to sit against, and one smaller than the eyelet to push into the bush. It is a bit fiddly to set up and is easier if you have a helper, but with the large socket positioned open end against the eye, and the small socket with the closed end against the bush, slowly squeeze the whole lot together and the bush will plop out into the large socket. Just make sure the sockets are deep enough to take the full length of the bush.

Fitting poly bushes to the wishbones can make a significant difference to the way a car handles, making the steering feel more direct and giving a quicker response to steering inputs, resulting in a more sporty feel. It's best to fit a whole kit to get a balanced car.

Firming up the anti-roll bar bushes can make a difference to the way a car handles in corners. The bushes on the anti-roll bar itself are usually the easiest ones to change, and can even be done in situ by removing the horseshoe-shaped bush clamps and slipping the old bushes off, cleaning up the bar, and slipping on the new ones. Job done.

Engine and gearbox mounts
It's not very often people think about poly bushes on the powertrain, but if you are an enthusiastic driver, stiffening these bushes can reduced mounting wind-up, which is the amount that the engine torque twists the engine and gearbox on the mounts when accelerating, and can make a surprising improvement in throttle response.

Most bushes are bolt on replacements, requiring the engine/gearbox to be raised a few inches in order to get enough clearance.

Make your own
For the intrepid engineer it is possible make your own poly bushes. You can buy poly in rods and machine it on a lathe, although it can be a bit tricky, and a very soft rod is best put in the freezer overnight first. Polyurethane has a

tendency to melt and chafe, so practice is essential before starting on the final item. Usual practice is to make a fast rough cut first, then use a slower cut to get a smooth finish. Beware; when it gets very hot it gives off fumes, so precautions are essential.

STEERING

As mentioned earlier, the steering rack was designed with a huge number of turns lock to lock: 3.9 for the power steering variants, and 4.8 for the unassisted models. Compare this to the Morris Minor, which needed fewer than 3, yet had a near identical turning circle.

There are a number of ways round this. One of the popular mods is to use the quicker rack off a later car. Here are some ratios for you:

Model	Turns lock to lock
E36	3.2
E36 M3	3.0
E36 Z3 1.9l	2.7

Using an E36 rack

One method of using the E36 rack is to retain the E30 steering arms by undoing them from the rack, then swap just the rack section, fitting short spacers on the rack-to-chassis mounting points to make it fit. This also requires the steering column linkage to be shortened, which, because the two lower halves overlap, can be achieved by grinding off the joint bolts and fitting new ones with a spacer piece. Obviously this safety-critical component should only be modified by qualified engineers.

Power steering

Power steering does introduce a small amount of vagueness to the steering. Some people prefer the feel of unassisted racks. Some people have tried simply disconnecting the power steering pump to turn an assisted rack into an unassisted one, but the vagueness largely comes from the valve block at the base of the column which is still present, so this isn't a great idea.

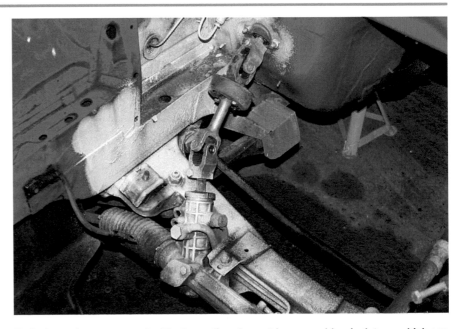

Typical steering components. The large disc element houses rubber isolators, which can reduce steering 'feel.'

The rack mounts onto the crossmember. Alternative racks can be fitted, but may require spacers.

Power steering does have some advantages, even in racing. By reducing driver fatigue it reduces errors, particularly on longer races. It also allows the use of very low ratio 'quick' racks that would otherwise overburden the driver. Interesting to note many modern Touring Cars use power steering. Contrary to popular belief, it does not sap engine power significantly, the steering pump is working hardest when the car is cornering heavily, and in this condition it is unlikely you will be using full throttle anyway.

Quality

There are a few companies making race racks for the E30, but as ever there are also some cheap copies made in far-off lands, which do not have hardened rack gears and may use inferior metals. Steering failure is one of the worst possible car failures to have, so don't take risks with the steering. Stick with trusted suppliers of quality parts.

Lower ratio racks can transform the car on a racetrack, but as the ratio drops the effort required to move the wheel when parking goes up dramatically. Fine for a race car, not so good for a road car in the supermarket car park! Again, it's a matter of using the right tool for the job.

The wheel

Another way of increasing the speed of response of the steering is by simply fitting a smaller steering wheel. Most aftermarket steering wheels use a separate boss that bolts onto the column.

In race cars, with everything positioned in just the right place to make racing comfortable, the steering wheel can sometimes make getting in and out of the car a bit awkward. To solve this there are quick release couplings that easily allow the wheel to be removed, which is also a useful security aid when the car is left for long periods between races.

The simplest way to increase steering speed is to fit a smaller steering wheel.

WHEELS AND TYRES
Wheels

If you are into modifying your E30, the chances are that you will want non-standard wheels, but I would just like to put a word in for those unloved standard rims. Firstly, they have been properly tested. In motorsport the stresses on the wheel can be very high, and regrettably some aftermarket wheels are not up to the job. Genuine BMW wheels are strong, reasonably light, and do a very good job. If you don't like the look of them then consider painting them a different colour, on a race car this can look very good and make boring wheels look a bit more special.

The quality of some cheap 'internet' wheels is truly shocking, there are no regulations requiring wheels to be tested for strength or quality in most countries, so anyone can melt down a few coke cans in their back garden and start selling their own wheels. Problems with cheap alloys include porous castings with bubbles in, making them weak and very difficult to balance. There are also designs with not enough strength which can bend or even rip the rim off the hub completely.

One of the few countries with a wheel test standard is Japan, any decent wheel manufacturer will have tested their wheels to this standard and have the approval logo, which is 'JWL' in a joined-up script, cast in. Of course there is nothing physically stopping a dishonest manufacturer casting this mark. Indeed, there is a growing problem with fake components, and this includes making exact copies of BMW wheels using cheap and dangerous processes

It is very important to buy from a good supplier who can trace where the wheels came from, and is accountable if there are any problems.

Offset

The wheel's offset is the distance between the centre of the wheel and the mounting face. A positive offset

The standard alloy wheels may be unpopular, but are strong and cheap – ideal for the budget racer.

means the hub mounting face is further outboard than the centre of the wheel.

The offset of the front wheels has a big effect on handling. If the wheel is too far outboard, every bump in the road will pull the steering, and when driving hard the steering will be constantly fighting you. Worse still, if a tyre has a puncture the extra drag can suddenly pull the steering wheel out of the driver's hands. A mm or two may not be that noticeable, but any more than about 10mm and the effects will be significant.

Rear wheel offset has less effect on handling, but if a large offset change is made it will increase the effective lever length of the trailing arms, affecting spring rate at the wheel, damping, and roll stiffness.

Wheel spacers

If a wheel has insufficient offset, a spacer plate on the hub may resolve the issue. But the stresses at the wheel hub are huge and the quality of the spacer must be high enough to cope. They also add an extra set of bolts into the system, potentially more to go wrong. It is far better to get wheels with the right offset in the first place.

Here are some of the standard offsets:

Standard E30 PCD 4x100, centre bore 57.0mm and M12x1.5 bolt thread.

Width	Offset
6in	35
6.5in	30
7in	24

The 325ix 4x4 system had hubs that stuck out a bit more, so the wheels had a greater offset

Width	Offset
6.5in	45/47
7in	41

The M3 had a 5-stud design, using parts similar to the 5 Series of the period. Some E30 owners change to E36 hubs, which is quite a big job – see the suspension section for more details – but does mean there is more choice of good secondhand wheels available.

M3 = PCD 5x120, centre bore 72.5mm, and M12x1.5 bolt thread. ET 27-30

TYRES/TIRES

Starting with the basics, the tyre has best grip when its contact patch is flat on the road. If it's angled over, the contact patch and grip are reduced.

This is a typical sports road tyre after a dozen laps on a race circuit. As the tyre heats up and the rubber softens, small strands of rubber peel off the trailing edge of the tread blocks. Most of the strands on this tyre have been picked up off the track from other cars.

Hard acceleration

Weight transfer can cause the back end to dip and the wheels to tip inwards at the top a bit. If you use really stiff tyres, the tread area will tilt over too, the contact patch will reduce, and you have less traction. If the side walls have a bit more give, the tread stays flat on the ground.

Hard braking

Now front wishbones move and tip the tops of the front wheels slightly, thus reducing the contact patch and leading to a slight weave at the front, and a greater chance of locking up.

Another problem comes if you start to turn in whilst still braking, which some corners demand. This means that at the rear, the camber has changed again, plus there is not much weight pushing the tyres into the ground, so we find the phenomenon of lift-off oversteer. If the back loses traction too much, it will swing round and overtake you shortly before you visit the scene of an accident.

So again, the tyre needs some flexibility in the side walls to cope. So far, flexible sides seem quite a good idea.

Cornering

As the car turns in, the weight shifts to the outside wheels, and hopefully the suspension cleverly compensates for the car leaning over and adapts the outside wheel's attitude to the ground, keeping the tread flat to the ground.

However, during hard cornering the tread is pulled over to the inside edge, peeling itself off the ground. So here a very stiff side wall seems best.

Now, you could compensate for the car rolling by applying more negative camber, thus getting better grip mid-corner. But this means that the wheels tip in more when braking, thus losing grip going into and out of corners. So a compromise has to be made. You can see how the suspension settings and the tyre choice are heavily interdependent.

The tyre moves under the wheel as cornering forces increase. The art of race car preparation is to set up the suspension geometry for this condition.

Another way round the geometry changes is to stop the suspension from moving. Indeed, purebred racing cars like F1 do have very little suspension movement. But this requires the road to be dead flat – any slight groove or rut could cause a wheel to lose contact with the ground, and thus traction goes out the window.

Profile has a big effect on side wall flex, and thus stability – the stiffer the side wall, the better the tread is held relative to the wheel rim. Car weight also influences profile choice: a standard E30 will force the tread on a low profile tyre into the road, but a 800kg race special needs a much higher profile to allow the tread to flex over the lumps and bumps in the road. That's one of the reasons F1 tyres have such a high profile.

So, generally a lower profile is better – but not so low as to stop the tread adapting to road irregularities. However, if you find the car lets go too violently, a higher profile tyre will make the break away more progressive. This may give you more confidence and thus improve lap times.

The design of the tyre will affect

how quickly it lets go – the more progressive it is, the easier it is to feel it going and drive on the limit, but it will have less ultimate grip. Generally, a more experienced driver can use the less progressive tyre to greater effect than a novice, and a novice should not necessarily copy the class leader's tyre choice, because you'll spend all your time spinning off.

Tyre size

A wider tyre can potentially generate more grip. The reason is a bit complicated, and there is not a direct simple relationship between width and grip. E30s are light cars, and do not really need massively wide tyres. The standard 205s are good for most road and trackday applications, 225s are a reasonably wide choice, and 245s are probably pointless unless you are running over about 300bhp.

The E30 is a very nicely balanced car as standard, and suits having the same size tyres front and rear. Very high-power turbo or V8 cars may benefit from having wider (maybe about 20mm) rear tyres.

The profile needed depends on the car's use, but again, the lightness of the E30 means 40 profile tyres are probably the lowest profile that a race car would need, 50 profile tyres may suit a fast road or trackday car.

As ever, check with the tyre manufacturer for recommendations, because all of this depends on tyre design, and tyre technology is always moving on.

Wheel and tyre width

Wheel width has an effect on how the tread is held, a narrow wheel will let the tread move side to side more easily, too wide a wheel and you risk the tyre bead coming off. As a very rough rule of thumb a race car would suit wheels an inch wider than the tyres, a road car may suit wheels the same width or half an inch narrower than the tyres. The best size varies depending on the design of the tyre, so it's always

Broader tread blocks are more stable, and so heat up less, making them more suitable for racing, but worse in the wet.

best to check the tyre manufacturer's recommendations.

Pressure

Tyre grip changes with inflation pressure. The exact relationship varies from one type of tyre to another, but basically there is an optimum pressure – any lower or higher reduces grip. Lower pressures have a more dramatic effect than higher pressures.

Believe it or not, you might not want the ultimate grip from all four tyres. You can change how the car under/oversteers by changing the relative grip front and back.

To fix understeer, reduce front tyre pressure. If minimum tyre pressure is reached, increase rear pressure.

To fix oversteer, reduce rear tyre pressure. If minimum tyre pressure is reached, increase front pressure.

As a bit of an aside, filling the tyre with nitrogen can give a slight advantage. The oxygen in air permeates rubber, but the nitrogen doesn't. Air is about 20% oxygen. Also, nitrogen doesn't expand with heat as much as air does, so the pressure in the tyre stays more constant through a race. This is a small difference though, so don't be surprised if you don't notice any difference in performance.

Temperature

Grip also depends on temperature. As the tyre gets hotter, the rubber becomes

Having wheels slightly wider than the tyres increases tread area stability. This can increase maximum grip at the expense of a more abrupt breakaway.

more flexible and can be pushed into the road surface more easily, but above the optimum temperature it starts getting too soft, and the tread moves slightly over the surface of the tyre.

The best temperature varies with the type of tyre, so again, consult the manufacturer's data. In the past I have used Toyo T1-R tyres, which are best at 80-90°C and go vague at 120°C. So if the car is driven too cautiously, the tyre will be below its best temperature and grip will reduce. Drive it harder, and paradoxically it will grip more as the temperature optimises.

Measuring the tyre temperature can be quite useful to a club racer. It needs to be done immediately after several hot laps – the temp will fall by several degrees per second once you slow down, so it's easy to get false readings. Even temperature across the tyre shows that the full width of the tyre is being used. Anything more than 4°C variation needs fixing.

If the middle is hotter than the outer edges, it's over-inflated. If the inside edge is hotter than the outside edge, the suspension needs adjusting (either camber or tracking).

Driving the tyre

Driving style is also heavily entangled with tyre choice. At a test day I attended, two top-level drivers took turns to drive one of the class-leading cars in our championship. They both put in similar lap times, but were using the tyres in totally different ways. One was braking hard into the corner then using hard acceleration, thus kicking the back out through the corner. The other was going into the corner faster, and almost pushing the front all the way through the corner. The first was wearing the tyres heavily, mostly the rears, and the second was wearing the tyres a lot less, but the front left was wearing more than the rears.

In each of these cases the suspension and tyre pressures could be adapted to suit their driving style, or the driving style could be adapted to suit the car. It all depends on which is easier to change.

Scrubbing in new tyres
Once past the release agent, new rubber is very grippy. But the heat of the first few laps causes a permanent molecular change, and grip drops a bit. Once the tyre has gone through two or three heat cycles, it is conditioned for the rest of its life and becomes more consistent and predictable.

That's why it is important to drive a few laps building speed, then come in to allow the tyres to cool, then go out again, repeating the cycle in accordance with the tyre manufacturer's recommendation.

If the tyre is not scrubbed in, a race car will get e few good laps in before the tyre performance starts to drop significantly.

Buffing
On a circuit racer, excessive tread depth causes the tyres to overheat due to the tread blocks moving back and forth. So it is normal to cut tread to about 3mm or less. As a budget racer I have always gone for 4mm so I get a little more use out of the tyre. The effect of tread depth depends on your driving style, too, if you are just starting and drive relatively slowly, you won't get the tyres so hot and can carry a bit more tread.

Buffing must only be done by

qualified companies. Ask other racers in your chosen series who they use.

If the tread depth is too great, you will find the tyres work well for the first few laps, but then the car starts sliding much more. The tyres get hot on the long straight, so you don't notice until you brake hard for the corner and fall off the track!

BRAKES
The E30 brakes are fine for everyday driving, but by modern standards are a little small, and on a racetrack they are a bit too modest.

There are three main approaches to improving the E30 brake: firstly, by making the existing system work better; secondly, by swapping in used parts from another model; and finally, by buying a big brake conversion kit. Whichever route you go down, it is very important to ensure it all works correctly, and to get the right brake balance between front and rear. For safety, manufacturers set the brakes so the front will start to skid before the rear locks up – this ensures the car understeers rather than spins in

an emergency. But brake balance is far more than just that. When braking hard, the weight effectively transfers over the front axle, and getting the right balance on a race car will make a huge difference going into corners.

Improving what you have
Much can be achieved by using the right pads and the right brake fluid, but if your brakes don't seem up to the job on normal roads, chances are they are not working properly in the first place.

The standard E30 brakes are small by modern standards, but with such a light car they are perfectly adequate for road use if properly maintained. Many of the complaints about poor braking stem from worn parts or partially seized callipers. Getting everything working properly is a good first step.

If the brakes are still inadequate for the project car, it is for one of two reasons: either they will not slow the car fast enough, or they fade after the first lap.

To make the brakes more powerful, you can use different pad materials,

Peeping out of the wheels, a nice set of race specification callipers provide significant increase in braking performance. (Courtesy Jim Cameron)

The standard brakes are small by modern measures, but can still be improved with minimal expense.

increase the disc diameter, increase the piston area, or any combination of the three.

Pads

There are some good pads ideal for fast road use, such as EBC Green Stuff, but getting the right grade of pad for the car usage is vital. Harder pad materials take longer to reach operating temperature, so for a road car that may need to work on a frosty morning they should be avoided. The heavier the car and the more powerful it is, the harder the pads have to be. Also, the drivers preferred driving style has a big effect on choice. Braking late and hard demands more from the pads, but gets them up to temperature faster. So what works well for one driver may feel awful for another.

The basics: performance brake pads, braided hoses, and racing brake fluid.

Grooved discs help disperse dust and gases, giving more consistent performance.

Discs

The stopping force depends on the friction between the pad and disc. Just as different pad materials make a difference to stopping force, so does the disc material. However, there is very little choice – basically it's iron unless you can afford the ridiculous prices of composite discs. There are harder and softer types of iron; harder lasts slightly longer, but softer has slightly more grip. More importantly, there is a variation in quality of the disc material, which can be crucial. Discs made with cheap iron may contain contaminants and other irregularities, which cause uneven heating of the disc, leading to brake judder, warping, and reduction in braking force. So, as ever, spend your money on quality.

Grooves and cross-drilled discs

Discs with grooves help to remove gases and any glaze that has built up, but only a few grooves are needed, if any. Cross-drilling also vents these gases, but often result in radial cracks forming, which can lead to the disc breaking up. In both cases the edge of the hole or groove must be properly formed with a chamfer to avoid making weak spots. There are a great many highly successful race cars that do not use grooves or cross-drilling – make of that what you will.

How big do you need to go?

The more power you have from the engine the harder you will have to slow down, but the downside of big brakes is higher weight at the wheel which gives the suspension a harder time, so again it is a matter of balancing each aspect to make the car feel right.

The stopping force depends partly on the disc radius – the further out from the hub the callipers are, the more leverage they have, but this is always limited by the wheel size. 280mm discs are about the limit for 15in wheels depending on the size of the calliper.

Another consideration is that when moving to bigger calliper pistons, more fluid needs to be passed through the

E30 model	Front size	Thickness	Hat height	Rear size	Thickness	Hat height
Solid	260mm	13mm	35mm	258mm	10mm	60mm
Vented	260mm	22mm	36mm	–	–	–
M3	280mm	25mm	41mm	282mm	12mm	65mm

Standard E30 disc sizes.

ABS is not allowed in some race series, but where it is, it does mean you get the best possible performance out of each front wheel.

system, so a larger master cylinder may be needed. If you retain the standard master, but use callipers with 10% more area, the pedal will move 10% further too.

Big brake kits
By comparison the Brembo GT M3 big brake kit uses 330x28mm front disks. Big brake kits can seem expensive, currently from £1500 to over £3000, so many people are tempted to use parts from other cars. One such popular conversion is to use the Brembo callipers from a Porsche 996, but as with any of these conversions they do not simply bolt on, they need an adaptor bracket to go from the mounting holes on the calliper to the mounting lugs on the car.

These adaptor brackets have to transmit huge forces, and must be made of the right grade of metal such as 7075-T6 aluminium. Beware cheap no-name-brand versions, which could be made of cheap steel or the wrong grade of aluminium.

For the more adventurous, there is always the option of adapting a larger brake system from a completely different car, though for safety reasons this must be done professionally.

ABS
ABS can be very useful on a track if it is working properly. It allows absolute maximum braking force to be applied to both front tyres independently, which is helpful when you are forced to run off the racing line and one side is on the 'marbles' of rubber left on the track. The standard E30 system is only a 3-channel system, so although the front wheels are controlled independently, the rear axle is treated as one unit. This is plenty good enough for most track applications as long as everything is in good working order. The weight penalty is about 2kg, so even on a lightweight 800kg racer there is negligible weight advantage in omitting it.

Later 4-channel systems that control all wheels independently, such as the Ate Mk 6.0 ABS system from a 2003-2006 BMW E46 M3 Competition Package (ZCP), can be retrofitted using a bit of custom wiring, or by buying an adaptor loom such as the one from Turner Motorsport, plus the BMW ABS pump/ECU, yaw rate sensors, ABS pressure sensors (x2), and wheel-speed sensors (x4). This is a costly solution, but does offer very good performance, and you can also get motorsport tunes for it that can cope with slicks.

Problems
Sticking brakes
One problem with sliding callipers is that the rubber bushing in the slider can allow the calliper to twist slightly under very hard braking. Normally for a road car this happens so rarely that it is no problem at all, but on a race car it can result in the pads wearing unevenly, and inconsistent braking, depending on how hot and pliable the bushes

Right-hand drive cars still have the servo on the left, but operated by a cross linkage and bell crank.

are. A solution to this is to fit metal bushing, usually brass, on a stainless high-strength pin. The downside for a road car is that more brake noise will be transmitted into the body.

Another problem that can burden budget race cars is sticking brakes. If using standard callipers, this may be because of the outer dust seals burning up and jamming the pistons. The simple solution is to remove them, but remember that dirt will now get on the

The biggest problem on the race track is brake fade from overheating. Ducting cold air into the centre of the brake rotor reduces temperatures. (Courtesy Jim Cameron)

The E30 provides a handy entry point for cold air. (Courtesy Jim Cameron)

And this is what the inside of the front valence looks like before the ducting is fitted.

exposed part of the piston, and will have to be cleaned off when fitting new pads. This seal must not be confused with the main fluid seal.

Airflow

Another problem with track or race use is that heat build-up can be excessive. Vented discs work by centrifuging air from the hub to the outer edge, where the wheel centrifuges the hot air into the wheelarch and passing air. This must be considered when choosing wheels for track use – they must have enough space between the spokes to let the air out.

In order to get sufficient cold air to the hub area, where the brake disc draws its cooling air from, most racers duct in fresh air directly from the foglight area of the front valance/under-bumper area. High-temperature hose must be used, as the discs can easily exceed 800°C and glow red. This heats the air around them enough to melt or set fire to most plastics. The duct can be bolted on a brackets attached to the stub axle casting, so it moves with the steering and suspension. It can terminate with an open end, but this allows some air to escape before getting to the rotor intakes. Another method is to terminate it with a fabricated casing that directs the air into the rotor centre.

The best setup depends on how much of a problem you have in the first place. For light track use, it may be that just opening a channel from the front of

the car is enough to keep temperature under control.

Fade and fluid

All that heat soaks through the system into the brake fluid, and although it is engineered to work at these very high temperatures, in extreme cases the temperature can get high enough for the oil to boil. This generates gases that compress easily and make the brake pedal feel very soft – this is brake fade, and in really bad cases the brake pedal can sink to the floor with very little braking force generated. Pumping the pedal up and down a few times can sometimes help, but basically if the brakes fade on a racetrack then the car generally crashes. And it's always a surprise when it happens, because heat builds during the last application then soaks into the fluid whilst the car is hammering down the straight, so when the pedal is pressed again there is nothing, even though it worked fine last time!

Old brake fluid absorbs water, which boils and fades much more easily, which is why fluid must be changed every few years. Silicon-based fluid is different – it doesn't absorb water, but moisture still pools inside the system and needs flushing through every few years. It's also a bit more squashy than mineral fluid, making it

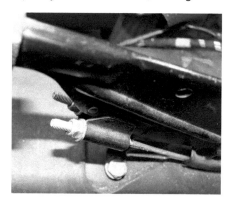

The handbrake has independent adjustment for left and right. If your racing requires handbrake turns (such as Autotests) ensure it is adjusted accordingly.

unsuitable for fast acting ABS. There is a misconception that fluids don't compress; well, they do – and this is particularly noticeable at the very high pressures that the brakes run at (up to 100 bar) – just not very much. Compressibility forms part of the DOT test.

The DOT number can cause some confusion. Many people think a higher number is 'better,' but this isn't necessarily so. The number refers to a test schedule with many features, such as shelf life, water absorption, and compressibility. It also includes fade resistance both new and after a certain amount of time, but race fluids age quickly, and so only pass older DOT tests. Some DOT tests are for specific types of fluid. For instance, DOT5 is only for silicone fluids, which have to be tested slightly differently as you cant force them to absorb water, but DOT5.1 is for ordinary fluids, so you have to be careful. Most good race fluids are DOT3.

Some manufacturers make fluid of the same spec in two different colours, such as ATE TYP 200, which is amber, and ATE Super Blue, which not surprisingly is blue. This helps when changing fluid, because if you use a different colour you can see when it has flushed through.

Personally, I have had good results on the track with Motul RBF (Racing Brake Fluid) 600, which is significantly cheaper than some of its competitors.

EXTERIOR AND AERODYNAMICS

If you are making a fast road car, the exterior look is largely a matter of personal taste, but a race car's exterior shape will affect aerodynamics, and even small changes can make useful improvements at speed.

Fit for use

When fitting aerodynamic parts, particularly wings, it's worth remembering what they do. Real aerodynamic parts transmit quite high loads, so their construction and

Whatever the external modifications, they will have to be up to the high aerodynamic forces experienced at speed. Even plastic windows can blow out on the track, if not securely fitted.

mounting points must be able to handle that load easily. If a rear wing is there to give you 100kg of downforce at full speed, most people should be able to sit on it without it breaking. Anyone can make a cheap fibre glass wing that looks good, but it takes skill and knowledge to make one that actually works. If you are going for aesthetics to give a road car the look you desire, the parts must still be strong – a front air dam will still encounter huge forces pushing it back at speed as it ploughs through the air. Just remember that a wind speed of 70mph is gale force 12 (hurricane)! Thin mouldings will flap about, and can eventually rip out mounting points. Badly designed panels can also generate unwanted wind noise, whistles, and groaning noises.

The E30 shape

To get an idea of the best ways to improve an E30's aerodynamics, look at the M3, which underwent a lot of subtle changes to make it better at high speed and therefore more competitive in racing. The standard E30 is usually referred to as a 'three box design' – it's slightly brick-shaped and doesn't have a great drag coefficient.

One area that causes problems at high speed is the rear window/boot area. The rear window is fairly upright, and generates a low pressure zone behind it, just above the boot. This not

The M3 incorporates effective aerodynamic improvements. Front end changes include air dam, splitter, and mirrors. The flared arches also compensate for the front wheels being slightly further back than on a normal E30.

The M3 rear includes a more steeply raked rear window with suitable rear pillar trims and boot modifications. The rear wing also improves downforce, and is balanced by the front end modifications.

only causes drag, but also lifts the boot and reduces rear axle downforce. To fix this, the M3 has a significantly different rear window, raked at a steeper angle so the bottom edge extends further

Replacement panels – such as this carbon fibre boot lid – can save weight, but if too flexible can be more trouble than they are worth.

The early light system is adequate for most applications, but can be replaced by the later units if desired.

Bonnet pins are required in some race series: the standard boot and bonnet fixings are heavy and are not considered reliable enough by some. However, sharp protruding pins like this are illegal for road use in some countries.

Later 'smiley' lights can be retro-fitted to earlier cars, although there is a change in the wiring connectors.

handling and plastic parts deformation. The air could also become backed up through the radiator, affecting cooling performance.

If regulations allow, it may be possible to stand out the rear of the front wings an inch, cut vent holes in the inner wing, and move under-bonnet components to allow hot air to escape through the sides. If the conventional bonnet release mechanism has been replaced with four bonnet pins, a simpler idea is to jack open the bonnet's rear edge half an inch. If that sounds a bit drastic, vents can be cut into the bonnet, but remember that if anything leaks or fails in the engine bay it could coat the windscreen in oil or obscure the view with smoke, so it's safer to put bonnet vents on the passenger side only.

Securing body kits or panels

Fitting GRP or plastic panels can be tricky. Often the mouldings do not fit exactly, and a degree of cutting back may be required. Where possible, it is best to bond panels to the shell with a long seam of glue, which makes a much stronger joint than screws or rivets. Usually, the panel is located with a few screws or bolts, but these can put high point loadings on the panel, which can lead to the mounting point failing. Therefore, it is usually best to put large load-spreading washers under mounting

The 'de-bumpered' look can look good, but exposes the front metalwork to any car park damage, and will affect aerodynamics, although probably not enough to be noticed.

back. It uses a unique M3 rear window surround. Also, the boot lid clears the new window, with a small wing to further reduce drag and increase downforce at speed.

This increased rear downforce has to be matched by a similar increase at the front, otherwise the steering would go light. The M3 achieves this through a unique front bumper/chin spoiler that incorporates a modest splitter at the lower edge to prevent air flowing downwards, and getting trapped under the car, generating lift. Similarly, if you look at the E30 race cars that did so well in Touring Car events, you will see a more pronounced front splitter and an extended rear wing.

So, the front and rear treatments work together to achieve correct handling. Simply putting on a large rear wing will improve rear axle downforce, but also increase drag, and may even reduce front downforce.

When considering aerodynamics for competition vehicles, it is worth looking at the underside of the engine bay. Most E30s have an under-tray extending from the chin to the suspension crossmember as standard, which is very helpful in reducing turbulence and therefore lift beneath the car. It's tempting to extend this to enclose the entire underside of the engine bay, but remember that all the air coming through the grille and radiator has to go somewhere – if it gets trapped, engine bay temperature rises, which can cause problems with fuel

The bumper acts like a mid-height splitter. Without it, more air can travel downward and potentially increase lift at high speeds. Also, the rougher surface can produce more turbulence.

A good body kit, fitted properly, can improve aerodynamics and make the car look very good, too. An integrated bumper/valance can save weight at the expense of collision resilience. The side skirts assist in preventing rear end lift.

points, and tighten the bolts minimally, relying instead on the glue to actually hold them in place.

If you like the look of the M3 flared arches and are thinking of buying some for an ordinary E30, think again. The M3 front wheels are set further back, so the front wings would rub on the tyres. Luckily, there are aftermarket M3-style body kits available that do fit normal E30s.

Paint

If your E30 is pink, chances are it was originally Zinnober Red and has faded horribly. Some of the colours used on these cars lose their shine quite rapidly, with red seemingly one of the worst colours for fading, first becoming dull then gradually whiter. In the short term, a good paint cutting compound can bring back the colour and shine, followed by waxing. But this will not last, and the only permanent solution is a respray.

An orange peel effect can be caused by paint being applied too thickly. Depending on model year, the sills may have been coated in thick, chip resistant paint, and will have a heavy orange peel effect as standard, but any other body panel exhibiting this effect indicates an amateur respray.

Cracking can also be caused by paint being applied too thickly, but it could also be due to the paint not being

mixed properly, or, more worryingly, that a heavy application of filler underneath the paint is cracked. In all cases it indicates substandard repair, and should be investigated. Moisture can get in through the cracks and start rusting the panel, so any repair must go back to sound metal before being built up again.

Blistering is very often caused by rust forming underneath. This is almost always worse than it looks. After the paint has been stripped, the metal will

need repairing before repainting. Small blisters on the wings are common on E30s. Sometimes a serviceable repair can be done with filler, as the area is non-structural, but this may only last a few years before needing replacing. Blistering on the bonnet, boot lid, doors, and wings may be cured by replacing them, but blistering on the shell, roof, door surrounds, and rear wings will need to be repaired, and may need welding. Tiny blisters of less than a few millimetres are caused by poor resprays, where moisture due to inadequate heating has settled during painting. These tiny blisters seem to come and go with changes in the weather as the moisture expands and contracts.

A permeable paint top coat and lacquer can also be caused by cheap car covers that don't breathe, and trap moisture rising off the ground.

Peeling lacquer is often caused by excessive polishing wearing down the top layer, but it can also be due to the bond failing. Early metallic paints struggled to hold the lacquer, and are more prone to peeling. The only solution is to strip it and respray, although a temporary repair can be made by

Front splitter, side skirts, and rear valance all help to balance underfloor airflow to make this car stable at speed.

picking off the loose lacquer and applying a quick spot of spray lacquer. This won't look great close up, but does stop the peel spreading.

Small dents can often be pulled out using a special suction device, or pushed out from the inside (if accessible), as long as they are on a flat piece of bodywork. Dents on seams or folds are more difficult to get out. Some experts may be able to hammer them back into shape, but it may be more cost effective to use filler. Either way, a localised respray will be needed. Similarly, creases and deep dents will need filling.

Large areas of paint damage and dents may be costly to repair, and it may be more cost effective to replace the relevant panel.

INTERIOR

The interior of a modified or race E30 has a very important role to play.

What makes a race car go faster? Power is a good thing, obviously. Suspension and brakes all help, of course. How about seat mounts, gear knob and steering wheel?

The 'office.' Strong and supportive race seats with good quality harnesses are essential for allowing the driver to have full control on the race track, as well as crucial for safety.

Race car interior

When you have a car on the limit round a corner, you sense the onset of slip, etc by relating what you see to what you feel. The more isolated you are from the car, the more difficult it is to be precise.

Ergonomics are very important. The position of the steering wheel can be adjusted by using the right size boss and by spacing the column mounting.

Having a very firm seat that is rigidly bolted to the car gives you the best possible feel for what is going on. When you turn the steering wheel on a road car, there can be a lag before the car moves and then the seat. This give a feeling of uncertainty, and if it's really bad (worn suspension bushes, etc) your ability to place the car precisely all goes to pot.

Now, this is an important fact: your confidence and precision depends on the feedback you get through the seat and through your eyes. It also depends on the car doing exactly what you expect it to, which is what all the suspension and steering modifications are for.

By the way, don't get confused if you see compliant seat mounts on a GT LeMans car – they need some isolation because of the rigidly mounted engine and rose-jointed suspension. Over a two-hour stint that would rattle anyone's nerves.

By comparison, the E30's compliant mounted engine and suspension means you are quite well isolated to begin with. So, for race cars, the seat should be rigidly mounted to the floor using the MSA compliant 3mm steel or 5mm ally mounting plates described in the Blue Book for cars racing in the UK.

The mounts need to be able to take huge forces in case of a crash,

On a race track, it helps to have something to brace yourself against. A sturdy left foot rest can help confidence in cornering.

Race seatbelt shoulder straps should be wrapped round the roll cage crossbar, preferably at shoulder height.

where accelerations of over 10g could have you bouncing round the car like a Nomex-covered tomato in a blunt blender. 10g – that's like expecting the supports to hold up the best part of a ton. The same goes for seatbelt mounts, too – the Blue Book spec for seatbelt mounts is 1.8 tonnes, and for seat mounts it is 1.5 tonnes. Imagine being able to lift the whole car up by the seatbelt mounts.

With the seat in your chosen location, you must be able to have a clear view of the road. I know it sounds obvious but it is surprisingly easy to forget whilst working late in the confines of your garage, you lose perspective in there. The balance has to be struck between mounting the weight of the driver as low as possible and being able to see the apex of the corner.

When choosing a seat, bear in mind that the E30 transmission tunnel widens significantly at the floor, leaving a relatively narrow space if the seat is bolted directly to the floor.

On the subject of seats, it is worth making sure you can't slide about, and that your shoulders are given a bit of support. That means you can feel the car moving directly, and can concentrate on moving your feet and hands without also trying to stay upright and in the seat.

Having said that, you must make sure you can move your arms freely to fully rotate the wheel in a mad panic (just try rotating the wheel whilst flapping your elbows, you will be amazed how many bits of car are in the way).

Your thighs should be supported so that your feet rest naturally on the pedals with very little effort. Try relaxing your legs completely and see where they flop – if it's in a reasonably good driving position, the job is done; if it's with your feet under the pedals, you have some adjustments to make. The more natural it feels, the less likely you are to miss the pedal when it all gets exciting in a spin on the track. It is quite difficult to change the pedal positions, without cutting and re-welding them or fitting a completely new adjustable pedal box. It is much easier to adjust the steering wheel, seat and gearstick positions. So, taking the pedal positions as the base from which all other parts are measured can be helpful.

Next we must look at the rest of your new office furniture. To get the maximum from the car and yourself, all the controls need to be in just the right place, falling to hand naturally where you expect them to be.

The steering wheel should be at a comfortable (but safe) distance, elbows slightly bent, but everyone has their own

Pedal heights should be balanced, and loose wiring should be tied back securely if the trim panels are removed.

preference – whatever works for you is the key here. When fitting race steering wheels, different length bosses can be used to adjust the reach. Some racers fit spacers between the column and the mounting point to lower the steering wheel. The dash and stalks, if used, should be clear of the wheel.

The gearstick should fall to hand

easily, and your elbow should not encounter any obstacles when shifting. If you need to modify it, make sure it is strong enough to cope with an angry driver putting their full force on it. The throw should be short enough for quick changes, but long enough so you don't get the wrong gear. Replacing rubber linkage joints with rose-type joints helps quicken gear shifts because it feels better and gives you more confidence. See gearstick section for more details.

Impact
Before finalising the positions of the seat etc, you need to check for clearance. There should be a fist-size gap between your helmet and the padding on the roll cage and any other bit of car.

Move your head about. If you find anything hard that cant be moved, it needs padding, and not with soft pipe lagging foam which instantly crushes – no, you need high density rubbery stuff. Genuine FIA-approved roll cage padding is a good example.

If you have a crash, your neck will stretch, so don't underestimate the clearances needed. Side impacts are the ones most likely to send you into a

For road cars, there is a wealth of interior options, using other E30 parts, or even seats from other models.

coma, so be very careful when checking B pillar clearance.

Also check for clearance to the steering wheel. Whilst strapped in with your helmet on, try to headbutt the wheel – if you get within a fist's width, you will hit it in a crash. I had a crash during a race which shortened the car by over a meter. Sitting in the remains of the car afterwards I tried the above test and could not get any part of my lid within 4 inches of the wheel, yet in the accident I hit it with enough force to smash the visor.

This is serious stuff. We want serious fun, but to have that we must survive.

Dash

Importantly, the gauges should be easy to read, even when you are not looking directly at them. In a race situation, your attention will be firmly on the road. In the good old days gauges had needles and were arranged so that all the needles were vertical when all was okay. We are very good at detecting horizontal and vertical lines, which may go some way toward explaining tartan. If the engine overheats or oil pressure

The M-Sport seat set is becoming rarer. Even slightly damaged secondhand sets fetch high prices.

drops, the needle deviates from the perpendicular and is easily noticed. This can be achieved by fitting auxiliary gauges and arranging them just below the lower edge of the windscreen.

However, all a race driver really needs to know is whether there is a problem that requires immediate action, such as low oil pressure, overheating, or fuel level/pressure. The best way to do this is with simple warning lights. These are excellent and work well using your peripheral vision, and lets face it, in the heat of the battle you wont be looking at the dashboard. They need to be bright and in a prominent position, such as on the top edge of the instrument binnacle. The standard E30 items are fine for road use, but can easily be overlooked when driving on a sunny race circuit. Bright LED warnings are ideal.

Air

Now that you are comfortable, well secured, the controls fall easily to hand, and your warning lights are sorted, we need to give you some air.

You need fresh air to your lungs to keep you awake, and also you need to be at a comfortable temperature. Give some thought to where the cabin air comes from, and make sure there is no chance of engine bay fumes or exhaust getting anywhere near it. A stripped interior is much more likely to let in fumes, as there are numerous grommets and seals that can perish, harden or fall out

Remember that the air coming into the cabin must also leave it at some point. The Saloon E30 has the cabin air outlet just behind the rear side windows, and draws air through the rear pillar, so it is important to ensure this path is not blocked by trim

Ideally, you want to arrange the pressure in the cabin to be very slightly higher than the pressure outside – only a fraction, just enough to ensure fumes won't be drawn in. So, when stripping the interior a fan system is still needed, with ducting taking fresh air from the outside. The blower must still be able to demist the window, too, although anti-

fog treatment could be used for some races instead.

ELECTRICS

Although the E30 is a simple car, there are still a large number of electrical systems present. All these cars are old now, and connectors are tarnishing and corroding, switches are 'carboning up,' and wires oxidizing, so at some point you will have to tackle the electrical system.

Additional circuits

Many modified cars have additional circuits fitted. It is vital they take their power feed and earth from appropriate points, and are not simply spliced into the nearest convenient wire, potentially overloading an existing circuit.

Things like additional cooling fans and auxiliary lights must take their power from a new fuse connected to the main positive feed from the battery. There is absolutely no need to cut into an existing wire. If a number of new circuits are being added, a small auxiliary fuse box should be installed with a common positive wire leading to the battery feed. Ideally, this cable should be as short as possible.

Take care routing new wires to avoid sharp metal edges, vibrating panels, or high-temperature areas.

The standard fuse box is prone to tarnished connectors – it's worth pulling out the relays and fuses for an inspection. Handily, there are often spare places for fuses and relays for additional circuits.

Battery

The battery could be located in one of two places on an E30: the engine bay bulkhead, or in the boot. In both cases, the main power cable from the battery feeds the car distribution point via an insulated stud on the bulkhead, which has wires connected on eyelets on the engine bay and interior sides. If relocating the battery for better weight distribution, it's reasonably straightforward to unbolt this connection and make up a new power feed lead, which can be run up the inside for internally mounted batteries, or under the floor as per the original 6-cylinder models.

For race and trackday cars, the large standard battery can be replaced with a smaller and lighter item, with just enough capacity to start a warm engine. For the first start of the day, use an extra boost start battery, too. The standard battery is designed to cope with starting in sub-zero conditions with heavy electrical loads, not something that is likely on a race circuit. Using a smaller battery can save about 5kg.

For better weight distribution, many racers relocate the battery to just in front of the rear seat area on the passenger side. Race and rally cars need the battery to be isolated from the driver, so that in an accident there is no risk of battery acid causing injury, or fumes causing an explosion. Battery boxes are readily available from race part suppliers. If the battery is in the boot or engine bay, this is not required. It is also possible to get gel-filled batteries that are certified for motorsport and do not need boxes.

Earth

Earth straps corrode, reducing the peak current possible through the ignition system, and also biasing the engine sensor signals. All this can result in significant loss of power and starting problems. It is often worth removing the earth strap from the battery, and cleaning up the connections on the battery and body ends.

Also remove and clean the earth strap on the engine. This has a hard life, and can corrode all the way along underneath the insulation. A corroded engine earth will give poor starting, and can bias the engine sensor signal to the ECU, resulting in poor performance.

If either of the earth straps appear corroded, replace them. They are dirt cheap, and there is simply no point in taking any risk with them.

Cut-off switch

For race cars, an electrical safety cut-off switch is required. This switch is designed so that if the car crashes, a marshal can turn off the engine and isolate the electrical system easily from outside the car. Traditionally, the switch is mounted inside the car so the driver can operate it, with a pull cable attached to an externally mounted T-handle for the marshals. This is tested at scrutineering before every race.

Simply disconnecting the battery will not stop a running engine because the alternator will continue providing the required electrical power, so the cut-off switch has three parts. The high-current switch is inserted into the

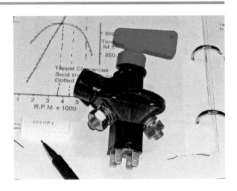

A typical FIA type cut-off switch. The large terminals are for the main battery connection, and the four spade terminals below are to cut the ignition feed and protect the alternator.

battery cable as close to the battery as practical. Below this is a block containing two more switches; one switch is inserted into the ignition feed, so as soon as the switch is opened the engine loses ignition power and stops, and the other switch is a normally open switch connecting the alternator power output to a 'dump' resistor, to prevent the alternator output diodes exploding when all its load suddenly vanishes. See schematic below for details.

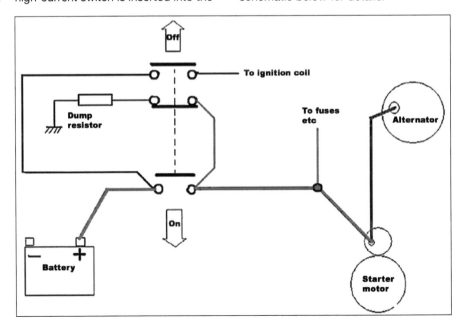

A typical wiring schematic for a cut-off switch.

For cars with the battery in the boot, there is a positive stud on the right-hand side of the front bulkhead.

The space is better used for other functions. Here I am fitting a push-button start switch and toggle-type ignition switch. The red cover on the ignition switch is a safety device which, if pressed in an emergency, pushes the switch to the 'off' position.

These days it is more common to fit an electrically operated switch, the advantage being that the high-current switch can be mounted right next to the battery, minimising the amount of unswitched cable in the car. The driver's and marshal's switches are durable weatherproof push buttons, and can be easily mounted in the most convenient place. This is particularly helpful on an E30, where it is very difficult to mount a T-handle pull cable at the recommended position at the base of the windscreen. There is very little metal there, and because of the bonnet design, in a heavy frontal crash the bonnet could come backwards and slice off the T-handle.

Ignition switch

Many race series regulations require the removal of the steering lock, which raises the problem of what to do about the ignition switch. One option is to carefully disassemble the steering lock internals and refit so that the original switch is retained, but many racers simply fit a new ignition and start switch panel.

However, it is not quite as easy as it seems, depending on how many of the original electrical features you require: if the car is a racer, all you need is the ignition feed to the engine and fuel pump; if it's a road car, you will also need the auxiliary function, so that the electric windows, mirrors and radio still work. Finally, there are two

A typical race transponder. It just needs a 12V feed to work, and must be mounted near the front of the car fairly close to the ground. I wire them into the ignition circuit with a fuse so I can't forget to switch it on before a race.

wires associated with detecting whether the key is inserted or not – this is for the courtesy function, which sounds a buzzer if you open the driver's door with the keys still in, and on some models it is also used by the central locking and security system. One way of tackling this is to use two switches, one for ignition and one for auxiliary functions.

The key-in function wires can be spliced onto the auxiliary switch input. Alternatively, buy a key switch with all the necessary terminals built in. These can be purchased from kit car parts suppliers, or from electrics component shops.

If the car is going to be used on the road, your insurance company will most likely insist on a key switch as a minimum level of security.

Airbags

Later cars with airbags pose a potential danger. Theoretically, if the wiring is cut open, a short to 12v could set off the explosive charge. For this reason, the airbag connectors have a shorting strip in, so when disconnected they effectively earth the airbag. So, if removing the airbag or steering wheel, always disconnect the connector – never cut the wires.

If the airbag is to be removed for a trackday car, the airbag system can be fooled into thinking that the bag is still present by fitting a 3.3ohm resistor in its place. This prevents the warning light

The later style headlight connectors for 'smiley' type headlights.

Old connectors are the main cause of electrical faults. Clean or replace as needed to avoid mid-race breakdowns.

coming on, and ensures the passenger airbag (where fitted) still works.

Dim dip

For a brief time there was a legal requirement in Europe and the UK for cars to have sidelights that also ran the dipped headlights at reduced power. The E30 did this using two resistors and relays which can burn out. The Dim Dip requirement was withdrawn after a few years, so this system can be removed in most countries, including the UK, as long as the car still has separate side light bulbs.

Engine

The engine connector uses a 20-pin round housing and allows some degree of plug and play between E30 engines. However, there were changes over time, so whilst I have found the following table useful on several cars, you must check it's correct for yours.

Pin	Colour	Function
1	Blue	D+ Alternator
2	Blue/Yellow or Blue/Purple	Oil level (static)
3	NC	
4	Brown or Brown/White	Temperature gauge
5	Brown/Black or Brown/Green	Oil pressure switch
6	Green/Yellow	12v Ign for diagnostics connector
7	Green	Ignition coil power
8	Yellow/White	Fuel consumption signal (to trip computer)
9	Black	RPM signal
10	Purple/Green or Blue/White	Oil level (dynamic)
11	White/Blue or Blue/White	Diagnostic connector (service interval reset)
12	NC	
13	Purple/Red or Green/Brown	Fuel pump power
14	Blue/White	Speed signal for diagnostic connector
15	Black/Green	Purge
16	White/Black	Airbag signal for diagnostics connector
17	NC	
18	Black/Yellow	Starter signal
19	Brown/Violet	Oil temperature (Only M3)
20	Yellow/Red	ABS 12v supply

The pin functions and numbers for the main systems remained fairly consistent, but the colour codes

The engine connector provides a handy place to splice in an engine swap or new ECU.

changed regularly, so do not take this as being correct for every car.

English	DIN (German)
Black	Sw
Blue	Bl
Brown	Br
Green	Gn
Gray	Gr
Orange	Or
Pink	Rs
Violet	Vi
Red	Rt
Turquoise	Tk
White	Ws
Yellow	Ge

Making connections

Splicing wires together – it sounds simple enough, but it's still one of the top causes of electrical faults. First of all, just twisting wires together and wrapping them in sticky tape is a recipe for disaster – cars vibrate and go

Good crimp terminals have two parts: one grips the conductor and the other grips the insulation.

through extremes of heat and cold, and engine bays get to enjoy an atmosphere of fuel and oil vapours, so not only will twisted wires loosen, but sticky tape will go soft, gooey, and unwrap.

A good connection needs to start with a solid mechanical join, such as a good quality crimp. The mechanical joint should be strong enough that the wire cannot be tugged out. The crimp must have two sections, an inner crimp on to the bare wires to make the electrical connection, and an outer crimp onto the cable's insulation, which takes any mechanical strain away from the conductor. Cheap crimp connectors only have the first section, and should be avoided. Getting the right crimping force is very important – too much, and the wire strands will be pinched out and break; too little, and they will have a high resistance and work loose. For this reason, it is worth investing in a ratchet crimp tool that automatically applies the right force. The alternative is to use the cheap crimp pliers and practise on scrap wire until you consistently get it right.

Soldering is another option, but as well as being a little trickier, it can result in a concentration of stress at the edges of the soldered joint, leading to fractures in later life. That's why F1 cars don't use soldered joints. If you do use solder, the finished joint must be wrapped with amalgamating tape or heat shrink tube in order to take the vibration and stresses away from the soldered section.

Sticky tape

Once the mechanical joint is made it must be insulated, both to prevent anything shorting out, and, just as importantly, to prevent moisture corroding the joint. It also gives the wires some strain relief. As mentioned, a good solution is to slip a tube of heat shrink plastic over the joint, which, when heated with a hot air gun, shrinks and seals the connection. You can even buy crimps that have integral heat shrink insulation plus a resin that melts through

The standard fault monitor can be temperamental, and should not be relied upon.

the whole joint, making a very durable joint. Another very effective method is to use self-amalgamating rubber tape, which looks like insulating tape but is not sticky. Instead it is stretched and wrapped round the joint, and over a minute or so it flows into itself, forming a single homogeneous, waterproof, unit. It's brilliant stuff and has loads of other uses round the car, from making grommets to fixing small air leaks; every tool box should have a roll.

Sticky-backed PVC electrical tape will not survive in a car for any length of time, the glue just gives up in the harsh conditions. However, PVC tape does have its uses, ordinary non-sticky PVC tape, sometimes known as loom wrap, can be wound round a wiring loom to hold all the wires together neatly and offer protection against chafing and oxidisation. Start by threading the end of the tape into the loom then winding over it, then wind in a spiral up the loom, overlapping by about half the tape width as you go. To stop it unravelling the final winding must be tied off by threading through the loom and tying in a knot. To finish it neatly the ends can be dressed in self-amalgamating tape.

Ever wondered what all those

terminal numbers on the wiring diagram mean? Well, here are some of the DIN standard terminal numbers:

1	Ignition
4	High-tension circuit ignition coil, distributor
15	Switch-controlled positive downstream from battery (from ignition switch)
15a	In-line resistor terminal leading to coil & starter
30	Battery + terminal, unfused
31	Earth return to battery
17	Glow-plug start
19	Preglow

Electric motors such as windscreen wipers

32	Return line
33	Main connection

Note 32 and 33 may have polarity reversed in systems where the motor has to go backwards, such as window motors.

33a	Self-parking switch-off
33b	Shunt field
33f	for reduced-RPM operation, Speed 2

33g   for reduced-RPM operation, Speed 3
33h   for reduced-RPM operation, Speed 4
33L   Rotation to left (counterclockwise)
33R   Rotation to right (clockwise)
45   Starter motor
49   Input to flasher relay
49a   Output from flasher relay
50a   Output for starter control (battery switching relay)
51   Alternator, DC Voltage at rectifier
53   Wiper motor, input (+)
53a   Wiper (+), end position
53b   Wiper (shunt winding)
53c   Electric windshield washer pump
53e   Wiper (brake winding)
53i   Wiper motor with permanent magnet & third brush (for higher speed)
55   Front foglamp
56   Headlights
56a   High beam with indicator lamp
56b   Low beam
56d   Headlight flasher contact
57   Parking lamps (in some export markets)
57a   Parking lamps
57L   Parking lamps, left
57R   Parking lamps, right
58   Side-marker lamps, taillamps, licence plate & instrument illumination
58d   Rheostatic instrument Illumination, tail- & side-marker lamps
58L   Left
58R   Right, licence plate lamps
59   Alternator ac voltage output, rectifier input
61   Alternator charge indicator lamp
71   Horn relay input
71a   Output to horns i & ii (bass)
71b   Output to horns 1 & 2 (treble)
75   Radio, cigarette lighter
76   Speakers
77   Door lock control

Switches, normally closed (NC) contacts & changeover contacts
81   Input
81a   First output on NC-contact side
81b   Second output on NC-contact side (no contacts)
82   Input
82a   First output
82b   Second output
82z   First input
82y   Second input

Multiple-position switch
83   Input
83a   Output (pos. 1)
83b   Output (pos. 2)
83L   Output (left)
83R   Output (right)

Current relay
84   Input: actuator & relay contacts
84a   Output: actuators
84b   Output: relay contacts

Switching relay
85   Output: actuator (negative winding end or ground)

Input: actuator
86   Start of winding
86a   Start of winding or first winding coil
86b   Winding tap or second winding coil

Normally closed (NC) relay contact & changeover contacts
87   Input
87a   First output (NC-contact side)
87b   Second output
87c   Third output
87z   First input
87y   Second input
87x   Third input

Normally open (NO) relay contact
88   Input
88z   First input
88y   Second input
88x   Third input

Normally open (NO) relay contact & changeover contacts (NO side)
88a   First output
88b   Second output
88c   Third output

Turn-signal flasher
C   Indicator lamp 1
C0   Main terminal connection for indicator lamp not connected to turn-signal flasher
C2   Indicator lamp 2
L   Left-side turn signals
R   Right-side turn signals

The standard diagnostic port is of very little use, although it does have its own engine speed sensor, which may be of use for ECU changes.

STRIPPING WEIGHT

It is easy to get carried away with stripping weight. The art is to remove weight without removing functionality, and to preserve weight balance across the car.

Basic stripping

The E30 is a relatively light car to start with, and does not have a huge amount of luxury equipment that can be easily removed, and often race regulations limit what can be removed. However, if you have the patience, and the regulations allow it, there is still a fair amount of weight that can be lost. This will give the brakes and suspension an easier time too. The standard 4-cylinder Saloon weighs about 1065kg, and the 6-cylinder from about 1180kg – removing 50kg is relatively easy, 100kg takes a bit of effort, and to get 200kg out involves structural modifications and a lot of welding.

But don't get too hung up on it. Roughly, most people would not really notice the effect of removing less than 10% of the car's original weight, so

The works M3 is a beautiful example of a stripped shell. Legend has it was acid-dipped to make the steel thinner and lighter, then strengthened only where needed.

what's the point? For instance, most door cards weight two parts of naff all, but many folk remove them and then find they have no way of shutting the door. Another one is mirrors – even motorised ones weigh less than 2kg, and removing them will make no

appreciable difference to performance but will make it more difficult to see cars coming up to overtake. So just remove things you really don't need, like the back seat, air con, spare wheel, carpet, and sound-deadening material.

Some people even swap to a smaller size of battery, saving several kilos. The standard one is specced to start in Arctic conditions, which isn't really relevant to a trackday.

The interior heater unit is another fairly heavy chunk, but remember you still need a method of demisting the screen on wet or cold race days, so you could replace it with a smaller combined fan and matrix unit as used in many kit cars. Electric heater units are available, which also save the weight of the coolant in the standard unit, but make sure the alternator and electrics are able to handle the high current these take. A 740 Watt heater is about 1hp, so it is unlikely you will notice the loss in engine performance.

Another option for race cars is to do away with the heater and apply

Carpets, sound-deadening, and standard seats are all prime candidates for the scrap pile.

anti-fog fluid to the screen on the race day. It has to be applied correctly to work, so practice is essential. I have used this method on a race car and found it surprisingly effective – unlike a fan heater, it keeps the very corners of the screen clear too, affording me even better visibility than a small heater unit did.

Either way, the demister function is a vital safety item and should not be taken lightly.

Plastic windows

The glass also weighs a fair few kilos. Side and rear glass can be replaced with plastic. Race regulations specify a minimum thickness, and usually specify the material too. Most racers use polycarbonate, which has trade names like Lexan and Perspex, this is a bit more expensive than acrylic sheet, but is much safer. Acrylic shatters in a crash and can form dagger-like shards, which you really don't want right next to your head and neck!

As well as saving the weight of the glass, fitting polycarbonate side windows also usually involves removing the window lift mechanism. Rally cars need an opening slider, usually only for the navigator, to receive time tickets. Pre-cut windows can be purchased with sliders built in, although they may seem expensive. However, once you have bought the correct type of plastic and spent several valuable hours cutting

At the other end of the scale, the budget racer is best concentrating on stripping only those items that will make big savings for minimal effort.

them up, you might find that the pre-cut ones are actually good value.

One problem with plastic is that it scratches more easily than glass, so care is needed when cleaning it (basically rinse, don't rub). This also makes it problematic for use as a front screen, where the wipers will eventually give the plastic a dull surface difficult to see through.

Sound-deadening

The E30 has a fair quantity of sound-deadening material added to the shell. Items like the bonnet sheet weigh very little, but removing them also removes a potential fire hazard, and there is no real downside, so you might as well get rid. The engine bay bulkhead has a pair of thick heavy sheets that also pass into the transmission tunnel. To get them out, remove the gearbox. Race and track cars have the interior carpet removed as a fire risk anyway, and again it is disappointingly light.

Underneath the carpet are tar-like sheets bonded to the shell metalwork. These are very difficult to get off. Heating them and using a very strong scraper works, but waiting for a very cold day and chiselling them off when they are brittle can work, too. Some people recommend using solvents or petrol to remove them, but I have never tried this because the fumes and fire risk in an enclosed space pose a huge

The roof lining weighs very little, but does get in the way of a roll cage. Sound absorptive matting is bonded to the roof, leaving strips of glue and fluff when removed.

Removing the dash allows access to the bulkhead sound-deadening material. Also, redundant electrical systems can be removed – there is about 20kg of wiring and electrical parts in a standard E30.

Door cards are often stripped out, but weigh very little, and do a good job of protecting the driver from sharp edges in the door.

risk. There is a lot of hard work involved in removing these sheets, so unless you really need to shave a 100th of a second off your lap time, the benefit is questionable.

By comparison, the headlining comes out easily, as long as you don't want to keep it and are happy to cut away the awkward bits. There are also foam pads behind the dashboard – awkward to get at, unless you have already removed the dash unit. Finally, the boot has some trim that can be junked or sold on.

All these parts are disappointingly light, but all these small weights add up and there is something in the region of

This heavy, tar-like sound-deadening is bonded very firmly to the shell, and getting it off is time-consuming.

20kg of sound-deadening in the car in total.

Cooling

The first thing to go is the engine-driven fan (see cooling chapter), but a lighter radiator may also save a kilo or two. Another consideration is redesigning the cooling system to use less fluid – each litre of water weighs one kilo. Obviously this is one for the professionals.

Exhaust

The back box and system can weigh up to 17kg. Replacing it with a straight through tube or fitting a side exit exhaust can save a significant amount of weight. Also, replacing the cast iron exhaust manifolds with tube steel items can save another few kilos.

Bumpers

The bumpers are reasonably heavy, and their removal can make a difference. However, they do protect the shell from minor racing incidents, and it can be better to have a slightly heavier car that makes it to the end of the race, rather than a slightly lighter car that folds up at the slightest nudge from competitors.

The bumpers weigh approximately 10kg, depending on model.

Removing the bumpers exposes the shell to possible damage.

Changing to a lighter battery can save several kilos.

Fuel tank

The standard fuel tank is relatively big. A normal 20-minute race is unlikely to require more than 20 litres, so a small lightweight racing tank could be an advantage, saving weight, space, and improving safety, as well as avoiding fuel surge round fast corners.

Wheels and tyres

Both wheels and tyres vary in weight for different designs, even in the same size. Selecting wisely can save weight and improve handling, too. Look at tyre manufacturers' websites for the data sheets showing the tyre's weight.

Big savings

There are relatively few race regulations that allow big changes, but 'silhouette specials' and some other classes allow unlimited modifications. If you're making the ultimate road car, remember that it still needs to be safe in a crash. Structural integrity is vital, and some of these modifications are not appropriate for the road.

A silhouette special class racer means that only the side profile needs to be retained, so all non-essential structure could, in theory, be removed. The roll cage becomes the main structural element, and extra bars are added to support all the suspension loads (check that the regulations allow this). This allows all the floor behind the rear seat, the rear bulkhead and boot floor to be completely removed,

with the roll cage supporting the rear crossmember mounts and the diff mount, and fabrication of an ally rear bulkhead to seal the cab from the road.

At the front, the chassis rails could be removed ahead of the front suspension crossmember, along with the inner wings and a diagonal strengthening tube taking the vertical loads into the roll cage A pillar, as well as mounting for the front strut tops.

All of this could save well over 50kg, but leaves absolutely no strength ahead of the front axle or behind the rear axle. All the remaining metalwork could be cut back so that, in a racing incident, the bodywork folding in would be unlikely to foul the wheels. Even so, it makes for a car with little or no crash resilience.

Also, it would be best to relocate the radiator, oil cooler, and other vulnerable parts to just behind the rear bulkhead for better weight distribution and safety.

Weight distribution

The main problem when stripping the weight out of an E30 for racing is that it is much easier to strip weight from the back than the front, which could potentially leave the rear too light to get the power down, reducing stability. Many RWD cars go for a 55% bias to the rear; NASCAR racers favour 65-70% rear bias, but the standard E30 actually has a front weight bias of between 50 and 55%. So, removing weight from only the rear can be detrimental.

Many models already have the battery in the boot, which leaves very

little that can be moved to balance the weight, so any weight added to a race car, such as the fire extinguisher, should go as close to the rear axle as possible.

Where race regulations allow, some people move the engine and gearbox back a few inches. It needs to be significantly more than an inch to make any noticeable difference, but all standard engines are fairly close to the bulkhead anyway. On M20 engines the rear water gallery tapping is the closest part, so the bulkhead may need to be reworked to accommodate this.

Once the car is moving fast, aerodynamics can help out, with a suitable rear wing and front splitter to hold down the back end. But racing starts and low-speed corners will always be a problem if you don't get the weight distribution right.

The other consideration for a race car is the 'polar moment.' If the weight hangs at the extreme ends of the car, when it turns a corner there is a lot of momentum to overcome. This makes it slow to start turning in, then once it starts turning it becomes more difficult to stop: put another way, understeering into a corner and oversteering out, with a tendency to miss the apex and always run wide. To combat this, race cars concentrate the weight nearer the centre, so rather than having the battery in the boot it would go just behind the passenger seat, the windscreen washer bottle (if fitted) would go in the passenger footwell, and so on.

BODY STRENGTHENING AND ROLL CAGES

The E30 has a reasonably stiff shell as standard, which is one of the reasons it has been so popular in motorsport. So for road cars and occasional trackday use, you could argue that no further strengthening is needed.

For racing cars the story is slightly different. The frequent hard stresses from on-the-limit cornering, braking and accelerating take their toll on the shell, and the weaker areas can start to fail.

The works M3 had the front strut towers tied into the roll cage, and incorporated a removable cross brace. Note how the driver's side strut tower also has an additional bracing tube to protect the driver in a crash.

The basics

Before any modification, first make sure the basic shell is sound. The floorpan rusts in all four corners, which are high stress areas. As well as repairing any corrosion, it can be worth welding in small gusset plates to spread the load in the corners and strengthen the area.

Suspension loads

If you are using very hard race dampers with spherical joints, the vertical forces on the rear damper top mount can lead to it failing, so welding on a stronger top piece may be necessary. The front strut towers are reasonably strong if they are in good condition, but can deform if you are running very high spring rates (above about 300lb-in) which can be remedied by welding on thicker top plates and joining them to the roll cage with a tube through the bulkhead.

The rear crossmember uses large rubber bushes. The body mounting point can corrode and become weak, requiring additional strengthening plates welding in. The rear mounting point for the rear suspension is the rear diff mount – the area where this joins the body may also need a strengthening plate on high-power cars. It is pulled down on acceleration, so welding a spreader plate above it helps distribute the load.

Roll cage

Collisions are very rare on trackdays, but many people fit a full motorsport roll cage. However, this itself brings new dangers. If the car is in a collision, having hard steel bars next to your head can result in awful injuries unless you are very tightly secured in the seat and wearing a good crash helmet. In fact, the cage must be considered just one part of a system that must also include the seat, harness and helmet, plus strategic FIA-approved roll cage padding.

If the car is ever going to be used on the road and without a helmet, a cage should be avoided. Cheap aluminium 'show' cages offer no crash protection and can fold into lethal razor sharp edges in a crash. If you are going to fit a cage, use one that is FIA approved.

Either way, the tubes near the driver's head must be fitted with the correct motorsport cage padding. This is a relatively hard rubber or flame retardant polystyrene foam to cope with the very high forces involved in a big shunt – using soft foam or pipe lagging is utterly useless. The padding must cover quite a lot of the cage, because in a heavy shunt your neck will stretch and you could hit parts of the car that seem very far away.

The fact that the body stretches and moves further than expected should

The bare shell shows how the strut tops and front crossmember form an open U-shape.

A typical weld-in roll cage, ready to go in.

Proper high-density roll cage padding is essential for safety.

Roll cage front members could either go through a modified dash, or bend round it, as in this case.

Critical areas that will need padding are near the driver's head, and where the door bar goes near the driver's leg.

be borne in mind when making any modifications to the interior. Avoid hard or sharp parts anywhere near your body, and don't forget the possibility of your knees hitting the underside of the dash (those under-dash trim panels serve a purpose, too).

For racing it's a different story. A roll cage is essential because a collision is more or less inevitable. Fitting a roll cage is usually best done before the car is assembled at the factory, what with it being nearly the same size as the interior of the car. Obviously this is unlikely to be possible here, but there are a few options. The most drastic is to drill out the spot welds holding the roof on, then re-weld it after the cage is fitted. Whilst this may be suitable for top-level race teams where large

budgets are available, for club level this may be too much work, and the cage must be fitted in pieces and either bolted or welded together in place.

The first step is to strip out the interior, seats, centre console, roof lining, and, crucially, the dashboard, which otherwise extends into the door aperture and restricts access. There are two options regarding the dash. The strongest cages have an A pillar that follows the A pillar of the car and goes straight through the end of the dash. The other option is a slightly weaker cage that curves around the dash. Once the cage components are inside, they can be loosely fitted in order to mark where the mounting plates must go. It usually takes quite a lot of jostling to get everything to line up, so be patient. Off-the-shelf cages often fit about as well as 'one size fits all' trousers, but if it *really* doesn't fit then take a few measurements to check the car is not bent!

Once it has all been lined up and the mountings marked, take it all out again and weld or bolt in the

mounting points. When dealing with the mountings, I try to imagine what they need to cope with if I roll the car heavily and the full weight of a bouncing car comes to bear on that point. A small plate could punch straight through the thin floorpan or wheelarch metal, so a wider plate of reasonable thickness is essential. Your roll cage provider will be able to advise.

I prefer to use L-shaped plates, welded onto the floor and up the sill to spread the loads through the stronger parts of the body. The floor mounts for the main hoop could also have a plate on the panel that joins the seat base to the floor for maximum strength. All holes and welds must then be painted. Remember, if you weld to the inner sill, the paint will burn off the inside and will also need corrosion protection.

With that all done, the next step is to put the cage back in. For a bolt-in cage, get everything loosely assembled first, then take up the slack in all the bolts, then do up each bolt fully.

The bolts in the wheelarch go in from underneath – that way, the bolt

Roll cage feet need to mount onto substantial plates; preferably welded in.

At time of writing, MSA race regulations require the harness shoulder straps to be mounted to the cage on a substantial bar. The easiest way is to have a horizontal bar of the same tube-type as the cage, which the straps can be wrapped round. Remember, the shoulder straps should be mounted at or slightly above shoulder height. If the mounting is much lower, in a heavy crash the straps will be pressing down, which could result in spinal crush injuries.

Strut braces

These have unfortunately become styling accessories, which means there are a lot of cosmetic items on the market that do little for body stiffness.

The first question to ask when considering a strut brace is one I keep asking: 'what problem are you trying to solve?'. If the strut top is moving enough to upset the handling, chances are something needs mending. Race cars running very sticky race tyres or slicks are usually the only cars that can put enough force into the suspension to justify a strut brace.

An effective brace will connect the

head gets covered in road salt and exposed to the weather, but the thread stays clean inside the car. Same goes for any bolts that go through the outer shell, such as those holding the seat mountings to the floor.

To install weld-in cages, the rear side glass and both front and rear screens must first be removed. With the members tack-welded in place, ensure everything is exactly where it should be – once the main welding starts, there is no going back.

Welding is best done with the car on a rotating body jig to avoid having to weld upside down. Some welds will be impossible to complete with the roof on, such as where the front cage meets the main hoop – it's possible to weld around about 320 degrees of this joint, but the remaining section is shrouded by the roof and cant rail. I have seen some cages with a partial weld get through scrutineering, but this does leave a stress raiser, and as well as being weaker than a full circumference weld they are more prone to cracking.

A basic cage will have mounts on the front feet, main hoop, and rear arches. Extra strength can be gained by joining it to the upper part of the car, too; for example, by using A pillar gussets next to the windscreen, and a B pillar web joining the old upper seatbelt mounting area to the main hoop.

A strut brace needs to be substantially stiffer than the bodyshell to make a noticeable difference.

The works M3 had electrically-operated cut-off switch and fire extinguisher buttons at the base of the windscreen. (Courtesy BMW)

A simple strut brace like this can still work well if tied into the bulkhead.

top of the strut tower to the centre point of the bulkhead, which in itself should ideally be braced to the roll cage. Alternatively, cut a small hole through the bulkhead and run tubes directly from the roll cage to the strut tops. Combined with the existing metalwork in the inner wing top, this forms a triangle and prevents sideways movement, fore/aft movement already being constrained by the inner wing.

A bar linking the strut tops has to negotiate the engine. Using a curved tube reduces its stiffness significantly. If the cross-bracing to the cage or bulkhead is working, it's questionable whether a transverse link will give any further benefit anyway. It also makes servicing the engine more awkward.

A similar argument exists for the rear damper turrets, although even if they wobble side to side a few millimetres it is not really going to effect the way the damper works, so you are probably better off saving weight and not fitting a brace.

Having said all that, there is nothing wrong with fitting a strut brace on a

road or trackday car for purely cosmetic reasons. If it makes you happy, go for it.

Seam welding

An interesting statistic from the era of the E30 was that up to 30% of spot welds were partially formed or didn't take at all. A common technique in the top levels of racing is to seam weld all the panel joins, although some race regulations prohibit this because of the high labour costs involved. A seam-welded E30 shell may be up to 10% stiffer than a production shell.

RACE SAFETY EQUIPMENT

Racing is dangerous – there is no escaping this fundamental fact. But to minimise the chances of injury or death, regulations and practices have been developed that prescribe certain safety systems and how they should be used. Most of the systems are partly dependent on marshals or other trackside staff who are trained on how to use them. For this reason, many of these items are not really suitable for

road use. If in doubt, there is usually a friendly race professional just a phone call away.

Fire extinguisher

If regulations require a plumbed-in fire extinguisher system, it needs a minimum of two nozzles: one in the engine bay, and one protecting the driver.

The engine bay nozzle needs to point at the most probable cause of a fire, which is usually any fluid hitting a hot exhaust manifold. But on an E30, the fuel system and brakes are on the other side of the engine, which poses a dilemma. The best solution is to use two nozzles with one on each side of the engine. However, this requires a larger extinguisher, too, to cope with the increased flow, so if you really want to use only one nozzle, it's pragmatic to locate it on the driver's side.

When siting the engine bay nozzle and pipes, it is vital to consider what would happen in a crash. If the hose is in an area likely to be crushed (such as the wing or front of the engine bay), it could render the system inoperative. Usually the system is routed along the bulkhead or strut brace.

Careful siting of the fire button or T-handle is equally important. If it is too close to the edge of the wing, again it could be inoperative in a crash.

The interior nozzle is there to protect the driver. It should point at the be armed just before a race. Although this is normally done in the pits before the driver gets strapped in, there is always the odd occasion when it gets forgotten, and being able to reach over and pull the pin out is in reality quite handy. Personally, in the E30 I locate the bottle on the trans tunnel, just behind the handbrake.

Battery box

As standard, the E30 has the battery either in the engine bay or boot, but for racing cars there can be a small weight balance advantage to be had by relocating it to just behind the passenger seat. If the battery is in the cabin, safety precautions have to be made. Firstly, to ensure there is no risk of the new wiring shorting out. Secondly to ensure that in the event of a crash or rollover, no battery acid can splash the occupants, and also to ensure that the gases generated by the battery cannot enter the cabin space.

To this end, a battery box is usually used. Standard boxes are available that already comply with FIA regulations. The box may be independently secured to the floor, but usually the battery retaining system also secures the box as well. It has a lid with a seal and grommets for the cables to pass through. There is a vent pipe that must be passed through the shell, usually through a grommet in the floor.

Cut-off switch (see electrical section)

The cut-off switch performs two functions: it isolates the battery from the whole car, and it stops the engine. An FIA-type switch has two main parts: an upper high-current switch connected to the battery and the rest of the car, and a lower double switch unit that cuts off power to the ignition/fuel system, and additionally puts a dummy load on the alternator output to prevent it from exploding when still rotating with no load.

There are two varieties of cut-off switch: the traditional mechanical unit

Typical budget plumbed-in extinguisher, with two T-handle pull cables and two discharge nozzles.

most likely source of flame – usually liquids or fumes coming in from the engine bay through the ventilation system, or through cable grommets that have been damaged in a crash. So, usually the nozzle is positioned to cover the bulkhead and dash area. It is unlikely the driver will be the cause of ignition, and remember that most extinguishing substances are irritants, so never point it towards the face.

The system needs two activation keys: one easily accessible to the driver when securely harnessed, the other outside, easily accessible to a marshal, and clearly marked.

The system also needs a clearly visible arming/locking system. Traditional mechanical systems have a pin on the bottle valve. This needs to be just about accessible to the seated driver, the reason being that it needs to and the modern electrically operated unit. Traditional units can be awkward to locate – ideally the switch needs to be within easy reach of the driver, but it also needs to be as close to the battery as possible. E30s had the battery either in the engine bay or the boot, making this a little tricky. Race cars often have the battery in a special battery box just behind where the passenger seat would normally go, which makes things a little easier.

The modern electronic units have the advantage that the high-current switch part can be remotely mounted from the control button, so it can be connected right next to the battery, and the switch mounted conveniently on the dash.

In both cases a second button or T-handle needs to be provided for a marshal to operate outside the car in the event of an accident. It is usually located next to the fire extinguisher switch, and the same safety considerations apply.

Breaking into the battery supply circuit is relatively easy, though, as in all cases the main battery lead connects to a positive stud on the bulkhead. This can be unbolted, the battery lead extended to the cut-off switch, and a new lead fitted from the switch to the positive stud.

The positive stud terminal also happens to be connected to the alternator, so the dump resistor switch in the cut-off switch can simply be connected to the positive stud connection above it, the dump resistor being inserted between the switch and ground.

The feed to the ignition/fuel system can be taken from the positive stud terminal on the cut-off, too, then through the switch, and cut into the normal ignition supply wire.

Rain light

Most race regs require a 'rain light' for wet races where spray makes poor visibility. Luckily the standard E30 foglight does just fine, but remember to test it before the race day!

Towing brackets

Rules have changed, and may change again, so check with your organising club.

The towing eye needs to be easily accessed, clearly visible, and large enough for a recovery vehicle hook to easily pass through.

Current FIA regulations require an internal loop size of 60mm, so either fit a very large ally towing eye sticking out the front, or fit an altogether more convenient webbing strap-type loop. Usually this is bolted to the bumper mounts and hangs just under the bumper with a clear 'Tow' sticker above.

Decals

Don't get caught out with stickers. Race regulations mandate certain sponsors' stickers, and prohibit others. Race numbers are like the number plates of the racetrack – if they don't conform to the standard format, you will get disqualified. Check the regs.

It is important to get stickers fitted properly. Small ones are easy, but the large sponsors' stickers and race number background can easily crinkle up or skew. The best way to fit them is to apply a generous coat of soapy water with a hand spray can, like the ones gardeners use. Get the area good and wet, then apply the sticker. You should be able to glide it into place and smooth out the wrinkles and air bubbles by hand, or by using a squeegee. After a few minutes the soapy water will have magically disappeared, and the sticker is permanently attached.

By the way, race numbers should not be displayed on the public road. For rally cars moving from stage to stage on the road, the usual method is to cross out the race numbers with insulation tape, the reason being it is illegal (in the UK and many other countries) to race on the open road. Race numbers are a clear indication that you are in a race, and the police will probably stop you.

Sunstrip

Racetracks seem to attract sunlight,

even when it's raining. Being dazzled by the sun is obviously dangerous. Standard sun visors may not work well enough if the seating position is lower, and if there is a roll cage, chances are you will not be able to mount them anyway. So, race cars usually have a sun strip over the top part of the windscreen. This is a sticker, and needs the same fitting precautions as mentioned in the 'Decals' section, especially as the windscreen wipers rub across them. Because the screen curves, if you just fit a rectangular strip it will curve downwards at the sides, so some trimming may be needed

The lower edge of the sunstrip needs to be low enough to prevent glare from a low sun, but high enough so that you can see the track, marshals, and the starting light gantry – at least two inches above your eye height, but this depends how close to the screen you sit.

Low sunstrips are not so clever on road cars, because you can't see road signs and traffic lights.

Catch tank

Many race regulations require an oil catch tank to intercept oil in the crankcase ventilation system. Normally the crankcase vent draws a small amount of gas into the intake system from the interior of the rocker cover. This is to ensure that the gases that blow by the piston rings don't build up to a dangerous level, and are burned relatively cleanly. The crank gases contain fuel, air and a fine mist of engine oil – quite a combustible mixture, so the system also has a fresh-air pipe leading from just behind the air filter, which dilutes the mixture, making it too lean to combust in the sump area. This is positive crankcase ventilation, and is fitted to all E30 engines as standard.

In a race, the system can become overloaded due to the higher blow-by and the lack of depression in the intake at full throttle, potentially leading to the sump exploding. (I once saw this happen to a Ferrari at a race at Donington – the explosion blew the sump off and coated the whole area under the car in burning oil. The driver got out just in time, but the car was totally destroyed.) There is also a danger of oil being drawn through the system and causing misfires or engine damage. To solve this, many racers fit an oil catch tank. The crankcase gases are taken into a container, usually about two litres in capacity, where the liquid oil can drop down and be drawn off after the race. The vent from the catch tank may be taken into the normal crankcase vent pipe to the intake manifold, but normally it would be piped in a loop, and either allowed to vent to atmosphere (which doesn't provide a positive draw on the gases and can lead to oily residue forming on the car in that area), or drawn into the exhaust close to the manifold using a welded-in tube. The latter has the advantage that the passing exhaust gas draws the vent gases out of the catch tank.

Harnesses

Accidents happen in racing. Usually they are fairly gentle because everyone is going in the same direction and there is good run off, but sometimes they can be severe. Every race circuit has at least one concrete wall. The pit wall has to be solid enough to protect the occupants from the worst racing collision. Concrete doesn't move when your car hits it – all the impact energy is resolved in the car.

Coming to a sudden stop puts horrific forces on the human body, so the harnesses are vital. Imagine a straight frontal impact: the driver needs to start decelerating as soon as the car does, so that the deceleration is spread over the longest possible time – any delay due to a loose seatbelt means that when you finally hit the belt, there is less time to decelerate and the peak forces are higher. I once raced with the left shoulder strap of the belt very slightly looser so I could reach the switches more easily – after a nasty crash I had bruising twice as big on the left side, so be warned!

So, the harness needs to be tight, but in order to work well it also needs to be securely mounted (see Chapter 4, 'Roll cage') and as wide as possible to spread the loads. Ideally, the shoulder straps should be mounted on the rear parcel shelf with large spreader plates, or better still, on the roll cage crossmember, so that they are at or above shoulder height. Mounting the shoulder straps lower than your shoulders means that in a crash your spine is compressed, which is bad.

The harness needs to be mounted so that the waist belt is across the pelvis, not soft flesh. A four-point harnesses can ride up, so most racers use a five- or six-point harness, which has a crotch strap. This strap should not press against the body – its purpose is to hold the waist belt down, and it should be mounted ahead of the middle part of the waist belt. On an E30, this puts it right in the middle of the floorpan, which is very flexible, so a large spreader plate is needed under the floor.

Dirt particles slowly grind away at the fibres, making the harness weaker. For this reason, race harnesses have a use-by date. It also means that secondhand harnesses should be avoided, because you don't know their history.

Race harnesses are relatively cheap. Buy the best you can – they save lives.

Chapter 5
Case studies

INTRODUCTION

There is nothing quite like seeing how someone else has done it to compare your own ideas, even if it makes you do something completely different. I have looked for a few examples of cars that really worked as a package, whether it's a full-blown racer or a practical road car. The ones I have chosen show how wildly different approaches can work, which I hope gives a broad picture of the amazing range of possibilities the E30 has.

PBMW Championship racers

The Production BMW Championship uses basically standard cars to offer relatively cheap motorsport. The rules are all about safety and ensuring the cars last, using the strengths of the E30 and addressing the weaknesses. They allow either the lighter 318i or the slightly more powerful 320i. Both make similar lap times, so it is down to personal preference rather than racing advantage.

Building on the E30's strengths, the engines must remain standard, and although some of the interior can be stripped the car must retain opening glass windows. In fact, it must be fully road legal and able to pass an MoT test.

The roll cage front legs follow the 'A' pillar and require a trim of the corners of the dash, but unlike cheaper cages these don't restrict leg room when getting in or out.

The suspension receives lower, harder springs and Gaz adjustable race dampers. The rear damper top mounts are also replaced.

Other revisions include fitting new standard engine mounts, cooling hoses, fuel lines, timing belt, water pump, clutch slave and master. This is to ensure reliability.

318is 'Ring master

Another great example of simplicity being key is the 318is used by Jaco Velders for instructing race drivers at the Nürburgring. The car laps consistently at about 8min 22sec, which is fast, but uses an absolutely standard engine with 143bhp. The secret to Velder's Porsche-killing lap times is small tweaks to the suspension geometry, and keeping the weight down. He used Powerflex polyurethane suspension bushes, a Weitech spring and damper kit, and larger adjustable anti-roll bars front and rear, plus spent some time setting the geometry just right (although he won't say what it is!). The car had 15in wheels with Kumho V078 semi-slick trackday tyres. This setup allows the car to corner very flat and quite fast.

The engine has just a performance panel filter and sports exhaust system. It doesn't need any more power, because Jaco made the car lighter. The shell was completely stripped and acid-dipped to reduce weight, and strength increased with a full roll cage and front strut brace. The very low weight and stiff chassis mean that he doesn't have to slow much for the corners, which in turn means that he doesn't need bigger brakes, which helps keep down the unsprung weight. To avoid fade, he uses Pagid race pads, DOT5.1 fluid and, crucially, ducted cooling air from the front valance into the centre of the discs.

Simple and effective – building on the car's strengths and changing its weak points.

Both these examples show how it is possible to build a very fast car by using the inherent E30 strengths, not focusing on monster horse power.

ROAD/TRACK 325I

The focus of this build is to make a car that is usable on the road, but clearly aimed at fun on trackdays, with a keen eye on budget.

The owner bought the car as an unfinished project. This can be a great way of getting a cheap car, but more often than not the reason the car is unfinished is that it's simply not worth it.

In this case, the car was definitely worth finishing. It came with trick suspension, a stripped out interior, carbon fibre boot lid and door cards, and race seats. Unfortunately, it also came with rust in the footwells and a mismatched set of wheels.

The basics

So once the new owner, Peter, got the project home, the first job was to get the

welding sorted in the footwells. Whilst the paint was stripped out of these areas the roll cage was fitted properly, with good sized spreader plates locating the feet. A new set of four-point harnesses is attached to the rear cage crossbar, and to eyes bolted to the custom seat mounting bars on the floor

The car originally had a sunroof. The heavy mechanism has been removed, and a carbon fibre panel fitted in its place.

Engine

The car is basically a standard 325i, the engine is a good sound standard unit and has been fully serviced for reliability. The only performance modification is a sport air filter.

Suspension

The suspension features an adjustable front anti-roll bar, so the stiffness can be set up to suit the conditions. It uses a set of 40mm lower and slightly stiffer sports road springs and adjustable dampers. The front lower wishbones have polyurethane rear bushes to improve wheel control.

The unassisted rack makes parking

The interior is simple and well laid out, with supportive seats and quality harnesses.

hard work, but frees up as soon as the car is on the move.

Wheels and tyres

The car came with some of the parts needed to convert to 5-stud hubs, but Peter wanted to keep the original classic look and decided to reinstate the original 4-stud setup with refurbished BMW 15in lattice wheels.

The tyres are ordinary 205/55/15 sports road tyres with full tread, which gets a bit hot after a few laps, but breaks away very progressively and allows for very controllable drifts on the track. Crucially, they still work well on wet public roads.

Brakes

Standard callipers are fitted with EBC Yellow Stuff pads and cross-drilled discs. Braking from cold is similar to standard, but once they are hot there is noticeably more stopping power.

Conclusion

On the track the car drifts in a very controllable manner, making this car ideal for a novice learning track craft, but it is also huge fun for a proficient track driver. It can be hustled round a circuit with reasonable pace and has, been known to overtake Porsches and exotic racers

There is a good balance between front and rear grip, so the driver can put it into over or understeer depending on driving style. The low weight at the back

A near-standard 325i has huge track potential. Here I am 'testing' it at Bedford Autodrome. (Courtesy Lee Marshall)

restricts traction, but this is perfectly balanced by the front anti-roll bar setting, which has been set to adjust the front end grip to match the rear.

By not over-stressing any part, it is a good reliable car that completes full trackdays without drama. It's lots of fun, and is quite acceptable as a road car too, although the roll cage is not ideal.

The great thing is that as most parts are standard, maintenance is cheap and easy, so this car spends the minimum time in the workshop and the maximum time available for driving.

THE 335

This is an interesting car, because it made the big leap from a track car to a race car. Not only that, but owner Jim used this mighty machine for his first ever race, at Brands Hatch in the pouring rain against a huge range of racing machinery including a Ginetta, hot hatches, and a race-prepped M3. Amazingly, he drove past them all and won! Interestingly the owner/driver Jim Cameron's day job is teaching people to drive tanks, which may explain how he drifts the car so easily ...

Basics

This car started life as a 318is, but Adil from A1 BMW Spares fame took the solid two-door, non-sunroof shell and fitted a 3.5 M30 engine from a 735i. Custom engine mounts allowed the engine to be mounted as far back as possible against the bulkhead. This also allowed a slightly wider high-flow radiator to be fitted.

Winning a very wet race at Brands Hatch. (Courtesy Jim Cameron)

This is what a winner's face looks like. (Courtesy Jim Cameron)

Both inner headlights are removed, the left one leading to a carbon fibre intake duct, and the right one being left open to help keep under-bonnet temperature down.

Originally the car was intended for trackday and road use, but Jim changed almost everything to turn it into a real race machine.

The shell is completely stripped, and stiffened with a full motorsports roll cage and strut braces front and rear. The driver and passenger benefit from very supportive race seats and five-point harnesses. The office is equipped with the usual race safety kit, including plumbed-in fire extinguisher and electrical cut-off switch.

Engine and transmission

The exhaust features an Alpina equal length double exhaust manifold that curves round the steering, leading to a custom stainless twin pipe system with a centre silencer built in two halves to clear the prop centre bearing carrier.

The flywheel is lightened to speed up gear changes. Other than that it's a reasonably standard engine, and produces 231bhp at 6258rpm, with a good spread of torque peaking at 245lb-ft at 4239rpm.

Gearing is still relatively long using the 735i gearbox and diff, but the combination of light weight and huge torque means that performance is rapid.

Suspension

Jim had the car professionally set up by KW, using height adjustable coilovers at the front and separate height adjustable spring platforms at the rear. Both ends feature dampers that can be independently adjusted for bump and rebound.

All bushes are polyurethane or solid for minimal compliance. Adjustable front top mounts allow precise camber adjustment.

The installation did not allow for power steering, so a fairly slow rack is fitted.

All the angles and corner weights have been checked and set to Jim's secret specification, tried and tested over many days' testing at circuits including the Nürburgring where the car is used to instruct.

Wheels and tyres

The standard 4-stud hubs have 15in six spoke alloys shod with 205/50/15 Toyo R888 tyres.

Conclusion

The tractability of the large engine gives this car a distinct advantage on track. Not only is the need for gear changes reduced, but it is also more controllable on the limit, as seen in it's very wet first race. Everything works together as a package, every modification solves a specific problem, and the result is a very fast and highly competitive car.

THE M3 TOURING CAR RACER

As a final example, let's look at what BMW did with the E30 in Touring Car championships. This was high investment engineering, and involved quite a lot of new designs.

The two main elements they used were the already reasonably stiff shell and the race-proven M10 engine block. The focus was on high power and light weight.

Engine

As previously discussed, the M10 block received the M88-derived 4-valve cylinder head to become the S14 engine. The race version used a larger intake and exhaust system, wider cams, higher compression ratio and full balancing so that the rev limit could be extended to 8200rpm, endowing the 2.3 with about 300bhp, and the later 2.5 with something in the region of 370bhp.

Shell

The 4-cylinder engine was selected for its light weight, and the complete car only weighed about 950kg in full race trim, including over 50kg of integral roll cage. The cage extended to the front strut towers through the front bulkhead and had cross-type door bars. That main hoop was tied into the B pillar

The works M3 in action. (Courtesy BMW)

with a perforated plate, By modern standards, it looks quite minimalist.

The shell was acid-dipped to make it a bit thinner and lighter, as was traditional at the time for all Touring cars. All the panel joins were seam welded.

The shell also had air jacks – one compressed air operated ram at each end of each sill. When connected to a compressed air line from the pits, the jacks raised the car off the ground and allowed rapid wheel changes.

Most cars had a racing fuel cell mounted in the spare wheel well, keeping the weight as low as possible, with two fuel pumps for reliability.

Only one windscreen wiper was used, which used the central pivot point, and its park position was straight up to minimise drag. The outboard wiper pivot points were used for other things: the driver's side got the cut-off switch and extinguisher, whilst the passenger side was used to mount the air line connector to operate the air jacks.

Suspension
The rear semi-trailing arms were re-engineered to reduce the sweep angle from the standard 15 degrees to 12 degrees, reducing camber change and toe-in change during cornering. As standard, the camber changes by one degree for every 28mm of wheel travel, so at about 40mm bump the camber increases by 1.5 degrees on the racer and 2 degrees on the road car.

Spring rates vary according to the track and conditions, but a nominal setup was about 350lb-in at the front and about 220lb-in coilovers at the rear (equivalent of a 500lb-in spring – remember, the lever effect means the wheel rate at the back is much less than the spring rate). Ride height was also adjusted to suit the conditions, but nominal values were 50mm lower than standard at the front and 30mm lower at the rear, maintaining the tail up stance.

Adjustable anti-roll bars front and rear.

The works M3 revealed. (Courtesy BMW)

Steering
Unassisted rack, 2.0 turns lock to lock.

Brakes
Front AP 6 pot 355mm by 32mm, Rear AP 4 pot 265mm by 30mm. Separate rotors on alloy hats.

Adjustable brake bias, twin master cylinders, no servo.

Wheels
17 or 18 inch wheels were used depending on conditions. The smaller wheels with higher profile tyres were used for wet races.

Interior
In the office there was a high back racing seat, a solid linked gear selector, an alloy accelerator pedal, and race gauges set into a panel mounted into the original binnacle. Cold air was directed at the driver's face.

The electrics were simplified. A set of circuit breakers replaced the fuses, mounted on the central tunnel behind the gearstick. Just ahead of that were the fire extinguisher and electrical cut-off switches.

Chapter 6

Technical specifications

There were many revisions and model variations, particularly for the M3. Here I have listed the most common variations.

Weight varies substantially depending on trim level, leather seats, air con, power steering etc. All these things add weight. Most of the listings here are for the base spec model, so actual weight could be over 100kg more in some cases, if the car is fully specified.

US models had larger impact absorbing bumpers, which add about 115mm to the vehicle length and over 50kg to the weight. Also, most USA models had a higher trim level too, which made them noticeably heavier than European models.

Convertible models were approximately 110kg heavier than the equivalent Saloon.

Touring models were approximately 90kg heavier than the equivalent Saloon.

Fuel economy figures can only ever be considered a rough guide. I have used the BMW published figures where possible, although testing methods did change over the E30's production life.

4-CYLINDER PETROL (GASOLINE) MODELS

Model	316	318i	316i	318i	318is
Year	'82-'87	'82-'87	'87-'91	'87-'91 (94 Touring)	'90-'91
Bhp/rpm	88@5500	101@5800	102@5500	115@5500	134@6000
Torque/rpm (lb-ft)	103@4000	103@4500	105@4250	122@4250	127@4600
Fuel	Petrol	Petrol	Petrol	Petrol	Petrol
Engine	M10B18	M10 B18	M40B16	M40B18	M42 B18
0-60mph (sec)	12.1	11.6	11.9	10.6	9.7
Maximum mph	109	111	113	117	122
Fuel economy combined (mpg)	26.7	31.2	25.3	27.4	
Weight – curb (kg) (Autos +20kg)	990		1065	1065	
Displacement (cm^3)	1766	1766	1596	1795	1796
Bore (mm)		89	84	84	84
Stroke (mm)		71	72	81	81
Length (mm)	4325	4325	4325	4325	4325
Width (mm)	1646	1646	1646	1646	1646

Height (mm)	1379	1379	1379	1379	1379
Wheelbase (mm)	2570	2570	2570	2570	2570
Front track (mm)	1407	1407	1407	1407	1407
Rear track (mm)	1415	1415	1415	1415	1415
Turning circle (m)	10.5	10.5	10.5	10.5	10.5

6-CYLINDER PETROL (GASOLINE) MODELS

Model	320	323	325i	325e	325ix
Year	'82-'91	'81-'85	'85-'91 (94 Touring)	'84-'87	'88-'91
Bhp/rpm	129@6000	139@5300	168-189@5800	121-127@4250	171@5800
Torque/rpm (lb-ft)	128@4000	151@4000	167@4300	170@3250	167@4300
Fuel	Petrol	Petrol	Petrol	Petrol	Petrol
Engine	M20 B20	M20 B23	M20 B25	M20 B27	M20 B25
0-60mph (sec)	8	10	7.4	9.5	8
Maximum mph	122		128	115	133
Fuel economy combined (mpg)	26	24.6	24.6	33.6	24
Weight – curb (kg) (Autos +20kg)	1125		1180		1280
Displacement (cm³)	1990	2316	2494	2693	2494
Bore (mm)	80	80	84	84	84
Stroke (mm)	66	76.8	75	81	75
Length (mm)	4325	4325	4325	4325	4325
Width (mm)	1646	1646	1646	1646	1661
Height (mm)	1379	1379	1379	1379	1400
Wheelbase (mm)	2570	2570	2570	2570	2570
Front track (mm)	1407	1407	1407	1407	1420
Rear track (mm)	1415	1415	1415	1415	1415
Turning circle (m)	10.5	10.5	10.5	10.5	11.1

DIESEL MODELS

Model	324d	324td
Year	'85-'91	'85-'91
Bhp/rpm	85@4600	115@4800
Torque/rpm (lb-ft)	112@2500	162@2400
Fuel	Diesel	Diesel
Engine	M21B24	M21B24
Number of cylinders	6	6
0-60mph (sec)	15.2	
Maximum mph	103	116
Fuel economy combined (mpg)	38	36
Weight – curb (kg) (Autos +20kg)	1195	1260
Displacement (cm³)	2443	2443
Bore (mm)	80	80
Stroke (mm)	81	81
Length (mm)	4325	4325
Width (mm)	1646	1646
Height (mm)	1379	1379
Wheelbase (mm)	2570	2570
Front track (mm)	1407	1407
Rear track (mm)	1415	1415
Turning circle (m)	10.5	10.5

M3 MODELS

Model	M3 incl Evo I/II	M3 Evo III
Year	'86-'91	'90-'91
Bhp/rpm	192-220@6750	238@7000
Torque/rpm (lb-ft)	170@4750	177@4750
Fuel	Petrol	Petrol
Engine	S14B23	S14B25
Number of cylinders	4	4
0-60mph (sec)	6.5	6.1
Maximum mph	146	154
Fuel economy combined (mpg)	26	24.6
Weight – curb (kg) (Autos +20kg)	1165-1296	1296
Displacement (cm³)	2302	2467
Bore (mm)	93.4	95
Stroke (mm)	84	87
Length (mm)	4346	4346
Width (mm)	1679	1679
Height (mm)	1369	1369
Wheelbase (mm)	2562	2562
Front track (mm)	1412	1412
Rear track (mm)	1433	1433

TYRES

A variety of tyres could be specified for almost any model, making it very difficult to determine whether the tyres on a given car are the original size. The standard sizes for all except the M3 were:
175/70R14
195/65R14
195/60R14 (only for M+S)
205/55R15
Plus the metric 200/60R365

OTHER BMW MODELS THAT COULD POTENTIALLY BE A SOURCE OF PARTS

TYPE	YEAR	COMMENTS
3 Series		
E21	1973-1983	Getting rare, and even the engines were lower spec than an E30.
E30	1981-1994	
E36	1991-1998	5-stud hubs, quicker steering rack, and useful engines.
E46	1999-2003	
E90	2004	
E83	2004+>	X3, 3 Series sized SUV.
5 Series		
E28	1982-1988	Potential replacement engines and gearboxes.
E34	1988-1996	Potential engine upgrades, some suspension parts for 5 stud conversion.
E39	1997-2000	
E60/61	2000	
6 Series		
E24	1977-1989	M30 engines.
E63/E64	2003	

7 Series

E23	1978-1987	Six-cylinder engines and gearboxes.
E32	1988-1994	Six-cylinder engines and gearboxes.
E38	1995-2001	Engine upgrades.
E65/66	2002	

8 Series

E31	1989-1999

M Cars

M Roadster	1997-2001	Z3, E36 Series based.
M Roadster	2004	Z4, E85 Series based.
M Coupé	1998-2001	Z3, E36 Series based.

Z Roadsters

Z1 roadster	1988-1991	Based on E30.
Z3 roadster	1996-2001	Based on E36.
Z4 roadster	2002	Based on E85.
Z8 roadster	2000	E52.

Chapter 7
Contacts

CLUBS, WEBSITES & FORUMS

www.thebmwclub.org.uk
www.bmwcarclubgb.co.uk
www.bimmerownersclub.com
www.m42club.com
www.e30clubsa.co.za
www.e30-club.de
www.e30club.ru
www.e30.de
www.e30zone.net
www.bimmerforums.com
www.r3vlimited.com
www.bmwboard.com
www.bimmerworld.com
www.s14.net

BMW SPECIALISTS

Munich Legends
www.munichlegends.co.uk

Classic Heroes
www.classicheroes.co.uk

PARTS SUPPLIERS

GSF Car Parts
www.gsfcarparts.com

Euro car parts
www.eurocarparts.com

Bilstein suspension
www.bilstein.com

ac-schnitzer
www.ac-schnitzer.co.uk
www.ac-schnitzer.de

CA Technologies International Ltd
www.catune.co.uk

ETA Motorsport
www.etamotorsport.co.uk

Turner Motorsport
www.turnermotorsport.com

Quarry Motors UK
www.quarrymotors.co.uk

Pro Turbo Systems
www.proturbo.fi

666 fabrication
www.666fabrication.com

RACE PARTS

Demon Tweaks
www.demon-tweeks.co.uk

www.raceparts.co.uk

OIL COOLERS, FUEL & BRAKE PARTS

Think Automotive
www.thinkauto.com/

Veloce *SpeedPro* books –

978-1-903706-59-6

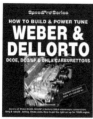
978-1-903706-75-6

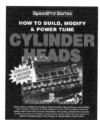
978-1-903706-76-3

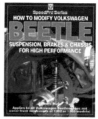
978-1-903706-99-2

978-1-845840-21-1

978-1-787111-68-4

978-1-787110-01-4

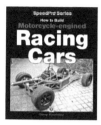
978-1-787111-69-1

978-1-787111-73-8

978-1-845841-87-4

978-1-845842-07-9

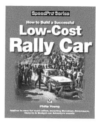
978-1-845842-08-6

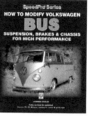
978-1-845842-62-8

978-1-901295-26-9

978-1-845842-89-5

978-1-845842-97-0

978-1-845843-15-1

978-1-845843-55-7

978-1-845844-33-2

978-1-845844-38-7

978-1-787113-34-3

978-1-845844-83-7

978-1-787113-41-1

978-1-845848-33-0

978-1-787111-76-9

978-1-845848-69-9

978-1-845849-60-3

978-1-787110-91-5

978-1-845840-19-8

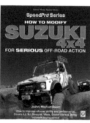
978-1-787110-92-2

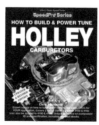
978-1-787110-47-2

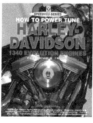
978-1-903706-94-7

978-1-787110-87-8

978-1-787111-79-0

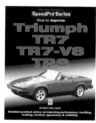
978-1-787110-88-5

978-1-903706-78-7

978-1-787113-18-3

978-1-787112-83-4

– more on the way!

DRIVING TECHNIQUES

David Hornsey

In-depth explanations complemented with diagrams & photography to assist all levels, from the novice track driver to the seasoned racer • Includes up-to-date circuit guides & detailed illustrations to complement the teachings • Designed with learning in mind, the book shows not only what to do to go faster, but also why these techniques work

ISBN: 978-1-845843-55-7
Paperback • 25x20.7cm • 128 pages • 100 pictures

A complete reference and learning tool for people taking to the circuit in their cars, either for the first time or as a seasoned campaigner. This book is designed to take the reader on a journey of discovery as you unlock the secrets of speed, from the basic principles through to advanced techniques and individual circuit tricks. Designed with learning in mind, the book shows not only what to do to go faster, but also why these techniques work.

For more info on Veloce titles, visit our website at www.veloce.co.uk • email: info@veloce.co.uk • Tel: +44(0)1305 260068

Index